School Power

Study Skill Strategies
for Succeeding in School

Jeanne Shay Schumm, Ph.D.

free spirit
PUBLISHiNG®

Helping kids
help themselves™
since 1983

Library of Congress Cataloging-in-Publication Data
Schumm, Jeanne Shay, 1947–
    School power : study skill strategies for succeeding in school / Jeanne Shay Schumm.
    p. cm.
    Includes bibliographical references and index.
    ISBN 1-57542-096-1 (pbk.)
    1. Study skills—Juvenile literature. [1. Study skills.] I. Title.
LB1601 .S37 2001

371.3'028'1—dc21   00-053569
Edited by Pamela Espeland and Darsi Dreyer
Cover and book design by Percolator
Index compiled by Pamela Van Huss

10   9   8
Printed in the United States of America

Free Spirit Publishing Inc.
217 Fifth Avenue North, Suite 200
Minneapolis, MN 55401-1299
(612) 338-2068
help4kids@freespirit.com
www.freespirit.com

Dedication

This book is dedicated to the best friend I ever had, Dr. Marguerite "Margie" Radencich. Margie believed in me and inspired me to do things I didn't think I could do. I miss her every single day since her death in 1998.

Margie was the coauthor of the first edition of *School Power*. She was a truly wonderful writing partner, a meticulous editor, and always on top of what was current in the field. In addition to coauthoring *School Power*, she was also the author and coauthor of many books and articles. Her work on the written page as well as her work in Miami-Dade County Public Schools, at the University of South Florida, and for the Florida Reading Association will be remembered for many years to come.

Margie and I not only wrote together—we studied together. We first met at the University of Miami while studying for our doctoral degrees. My wish for all my readers is that you, too, can find a supportive study buddy like Margie.

Acknowledgments

Because *School Power* is a book for middle-school students, several students your age were involved with the development of the book. Each of the Advisory Board members provided great suggestions! I want to thank each one for their time and for their comments: John Klingner, Miami Shores, Florida; Kate Post, Miami, Florida; Jeff Shay, Pembroke Pines, Florida; Kyle Shay, Pembroke Pines, Florida; and Charlie Watkins, Miami, Florida. An additional thanks to Alyssa Clevenger for her expert assistance in the preparation of this manuscript.

Some of the information in Listen and Take Notes on pages 23–33 originally appeared in "An 8-Step Instructional Plan for Teaching Note-Taking Skills to Middle School Students," by Jeanne Shay Schumm and K. Lopate (*Florida Reading Quarterly,* 1989).

The Cornell note-taking system on pages 26–28 was originally described in *How to Study in College* by Walter Pauk, now in its seventh edition (Boston: Houghton Mifflin, 2000).

The FLIP strategy on pages 45–47 is adapted from "FLIP: A Framework for Content Area Reading," by Jeanne Shay Schumm and C.T. Mangrum, (*Journal of Reading* 35, 1991: 120–124).

The All About Whales semantic mapping example on page 54 is from *The Semantic Mapper* by Gloria Kuchinskas and Marguerite C. Radencich (Gainesville, FL: Teacher Support Software, 1986). Reprinted with permission from Teacher Support Software.

Marc's First Draft, Revisions, Edits, and Final Draft on pages 67, 68, 69, and 70 are used with permission from Renee Flash.

The A-OK strategy on pages 68–70 is adapted with permission from "A-OK: A Reading for Revision Strategy," by Jeanne Shay Schumm (*Reading: Exploration and Discovery,* Vol. 10, No. 1, Fall 1987).

The PORPE strategy on page 92 was originally described in "PORPE: A Writing Strategy for Studying and Learning in the Content Areas," by M.L. Simpson (*Journal of Reading* 29, 1974: 407–414).

The STAR strategy on page 93 was originally described in "S.T.A.R., a Strategy for Taking Timed Tests," by Marguerite C. Radencich (*Forum for Reading* 17, Fall/Winter 1985: 29–34).

Spelling Demons and Spelling Demons II on pages 128 and 129 are adapted from *The Reading Teacher's Book of Lists* by Edward B. Fry, Jacqueline E. Kress, and Dona Lee Fountoukidis (Englewood Cliffs, NJ: Prentice Hall, 2000).

Contents

Tools for School Success 99

Index 131

About the Author 136

Introduction

If you're busy adjusting to life in middle school/junior high—getting used to changing classes, coping with different teachers' styles and rules, following a schedule that can be confusing—*School Power* is for you. Even if you're not in middle school, it will help you make it through whatever grade you're in.

This isn't an ordinary school book or textbook. It's a how-to guide for just about everything you need to know to succeed in school. Would you like to be able to read faster? See pages 49–51. Would you like to take better notes in class? Check out pages 24–32. Do you hate to write? Turn to page 63. Do you lose track of long-range projects? Find help on pages 19–20. Is it hard for you to talk to your teachers? See page 16 for suggestions. Scan the Contents and the Index; they'll point you toward the tips, techniques, and strategies you need.

Keep this guide handy every day—on your desk, with your textbooks, anywhere within easy reach. Stick it in your backpack along with your daily homework assignments. Write notes in it, highlight important points, mark key pages with colored clips or self-stick notes (except for if you checked out this book from the library—never write in a library book!). Turn to it whenever you need to review an important procedure or tackle a problem. Use it regularly and you'll find school getting easier, more manageable—maybe even more fun.

Get Your Act Together

ORGANIZE YOUR LIFE

When you were in the lower grades, organizing your life was easy. Why? Because you didn't have to do it! Your parents probably organized your time at home. Your teacher structured your time at school. Now it's up to *you* to keep track of your tasks and activities.

Organizing your life can improve your success in school, help you avoid last-minute cram-a-thons, and help you persuade teachers and parents that you're becoming more mature and independent. You'll earn more privileges and freedom.

How to ➤ Set Up a Home Study Center

Some people can study in the middle of blaring TVs and radios, ringing phones, battling brothers and sisters, barking family dogs, and busy parents shuffling around. Maybe you're one of these people, but probably you're not. Use the following guidelines to help you study better.

Location: Try to find a quiet place that's free from distractions (no phone, no video games). Choose a place where you don't do other things. For example, if you study on your bed, you'll start thinking about falling asleep, and pretty soon . . . zzzzzz.

Lighting: Some students like it bright, while others choose softer lighting. Natural light is best for you, but whatever light you use, make sure there's enough to read and work without straining your eyes. A lamp should shed light over your shoulder. It should not be aimed straight at the printed page.

Seating: It's okay to slump into a beanbag chair to read a story. But when you really need to concentrate, try a straight-backed chair at a table or desk.

Noise: Try to pick a place away from the center of activity. Post a personalized DO NOT DISTURB sign to let others know you're working.

Supplies: Many students waste valuable time searching for study supplies. You can be more efficient. Keep these things handy on your desk, in a shoebox, or in a plastic bag.

✔ pencils	✔ hole punch	✔ paper clips
✔ pens	✔ pencil sharpener	✔ index cards
✔ erasers	✔ glue or paste	✔ calculator
✔ markers	✔ stapler	✔ (anything else?)
✔ writing paper	✔ ruler	
✔ tape	✔ colored pencils	

Stocking a study center can get expensive. If there's something you need and don't have, talk it over with your teachers. They may have extra supplies on hand.

John's Tip for Setting Up a Home Study Center

My mom and dad think it's important for me to learn how to manage a budget. This year I had a budget for my birthday party. I had to plan the party within the amount of money my parents gave me. If I wanted to spend more, I had to use my own money. I recommend this idea for setting up a home study center and buying school supplies at the beginning of each semester. Find out what your teachers require, estimate how much it will cost, and work out a budget with your family.

Computer: More and more home study centers include a computer, a printer, and, in some cases, a scanner. However, the computer usually isn't in a student's personal study center, but rather in a space shared with other family members. If this is the case at your home, you'll have to plan ahead, so you aren't wanting to use the computer at the same time as someone else in your family.

Storage for Long-Range Projects: Some projects for school can take weeks or months to finish. Research projects and science fair projects often are long-range, and they not only involve a lot of time but a lot of space as well. In planning for long-range projects, think about how to organize the materials you'll need for the project. Perhaps you'll need some filing space. You might need plastic bins to hold books, experiment equipment, or art supplies. Keeping all of your equipment and materials for projects in one space will help keep you—and the project—organized. Bits and pieces won't be scattered all over your room—or all over the house. A visit to a housewares store or to a specialty store can give you some ideas.

Continues on next page >>

References: Build a small personal library with at least a dictionary and a thesaurus. Also useful: a one-volume desk encyclopedia, a set of encyclopedias (if your family has one), or access to an online encyclopedia. Add an almanac, an atlas, and other references as you need them. If you're taking a foreign language, you'll probably want a special dictionary, for example, a Spanish-English dictionary.

Bulletin Board: Use a bulletin board to post calendars, important notices, and directions for special projects. Leave room for postcards, pictures, and cartoons. Your study center doesn't have to be boring!

Michelle's Tip for Students on the Go

Michelle is a competitive swimmer who practices 20 hours a week and goes to swim meets on a regular basis. To keep up with her school work, she keeps a "study kit" in the family car. This kit includes many of the items on the list of supplies (see page 4)—plus a lapboard. This allows Michelle to study in the car on her way to and from practices and at meets while she's waiting for her event.

What If You Don't Have a Home Computer?

Having a home computer is convenient. However, many families don't have a home computer. Other families might have many family members sharing one computer. And, of course, there are times when the computer breaks down and won't do what needs to be done. Here are some suggestions for when computer access is difficult:

> Ask your teacher about using the classroom computer before or after school.

> Check with your school computer lab or media center about the availability of computers before and after school.

> Check community resources such as the Boys and Girls Clubs, YMCA, local community center, or public library. They may have computers you can use and may also offer short classes to help you learn how to use a computer.

> Talk to your school counselor. Your counselor may know of programs available through the school (such as school/business partnerships) that sponsor purchasing home computers for students.

> Ask your parents about talking to a neighbor or close family friend about "bartering" to use a computer. For example, you might mow a lawn or provide baby-sitting services for computer time on your friend's computer.

> Start saving. Computers are becoming less and less expensive. Perhaps your parents might work out a cost-sharing plan—they pay for part; you pay for part.

> Above all, don't use the lack of computer access as an excuse for not getting your work done. Talk with your teacher about your computer situation and make certain that you have a plan for completing your work with or without a computer at your fingertips!

How to → Organize Your Learning Environment

Keep It Simple

The more you have to keep track of, the more likely you are to lose something. Before you add another notebook, bookbag, or backpack, ask yourself, "Do I *really* need this?"

Prevent learning-environment pollution. Backpacks, bookbags, notebooks, and lockers can become catchalls, garbage dumps, and toxic waste sites.

Backpacks, Bookbags, and Notebooks

→ If you throw things in your backpack, bookbag, or notebook all day long, start your after-school studies with a five-minute cleanup.

→ Each night before you go to bed, make sure you have everything you need for the next day stored in your backpack or bookbag ready to go. Leave it all in a convenient, regular place for pickup in the morning. Also, spend about five minutes cleaning up your study center.

Lockers

→ Trash those old papers, bologna sandwiches, and smelly P.E. sneakers. Post a copy of your daily schedule (see page 10) inside the door.

How to → Organize Your Time

Planning Calendars and Assignment Notebooks

A planning calendar or an assignment notebook is a must. Carry it with you to all of your classes, tutoring sessions, and club meetings.

Use your calendar or assignment notebook to record due dates for homework, appointments (doctor, dentist, etc.), practices, lesson times, birthdays, special events, and vacations. About once every month, check your calendar against your family's schedule so you can record upcoming events and avoid conflicts.

- You don't need to buy an expensive calendar. Businesses often give away free pocket planning calendars for advertising purposes.

- Some middle schools print planning calendars for all students. These calendars include all major school events and holidays.

- Many middle-school students like to use teacher planning calendars, available in school and office supply stores. Some of these come three-hole-punched to go in a loose-leaf notebook.

- You can also find special student calendars with "to do" lists and pages for recording assignments.

- Calendars and "to do" list formats can also be found online (see for example, *calendar.yahoo.com*).

In addition to your local office supply stores, here are some companies that sell student calendars:

The AT-A-GLANCE Group
101 O'Neil Road
Sidney, NY 13838-1099
1-888-205-3324

Day-Timers, Inc.
1 Willow Lane
East Texas, PA 18046
1-800-805-2615

Franklin Covey
2200 West Parkway Blvd.
Salt Lake City, UT 84119
1-800-819-1812

Continues on next page))

Wall Calendars: Some students like to get the big picture by posting a wall calendar in their home study center or locker. They use it to jot down major events and deadlines. Life is more complicated if you keep two calendars. But if a wall calendar works for you, use one.

	Monday	Tuesday	Wednesday	Thursday	Friday	Saturday	Sunday
8:00	Math	Math	Math	Math	Math		
9:00	Science	Art	Science	Art	Science		
10:00	Vocabulary/ Reading	Vocabulary/ Reading	Vocabulary/ Reading	Vocabulary/ Reading	Vocabulary/ Reading	Sca	
11:00	Lunch	Lunch	Lunch	Lunch	Lunch		
12:00	Social Studies	Music	Social Studies	Music	Social Studies	Lun	
1:00	Library Skills	Spanish	Library Skills	Spanish	Library Skills	Bask Go	
2:00	P.E.	P.E.	P.E.	P.E.	P.E.		
3:00	Basketball Practice	Car Pool SNACK!	Basketball Practice	Car Pool SNACK!	Car Pool SNACK!		
4:00		Home- work		Home- work	FREE Time!		
5:00	Car Pool Home- work	FREE Time!	Car Pool Home- work	FREE Time!			
6:00	Dinner	Dinner	Dinner	Dinner	Dinner		
7:00	Home- work	Home- work	Home- work	Home- work	Play Practice		
8:00	Homework or TV	Homework or TV	Homework or TV	Homework or TV			
9:00	TV/ Shower	TV/ Shower	TV/ Shower	TV/ Shower			
10:00	Bed	Bed	Bed	Bed	Bed		

Nick's Schedule

Nick is in eighth grade. He enjoys sports and is on his school's basketball team. He's also an actor in community theater. Recently, he starred in a production of *Oliver*. Nick has a busy schedule, but he still manages to keep up with his homework *and* have some free time. Here's how he does it.

Daily Schedules: Keeping track of your daily schedule is easy when you use a time management chart. See page 100 for a blank time management chart you can copy and use.

- Start by writing in all of your regularly scheduled activities (classes, band practice, soccer practice, piano lessons).
- Next, block out your homework time (math, reading, study time for tests).
- Add your daily living activities (meals, sleep, chores).
- Chart your personal time (TV, recreation, relaxation, friends).

Make copies of your time management chart for your notebook, your locker at school, and your bulletin board at home. Revise your chart whenever there's a change in your regularly scheduled activities.

Time Management Tips

Set Priorities

If you have lots to do, make a list of everything, then rank each task in A-B-C order. Do the A task first, the B task second, and so on down through your list. You'll worry less and get more accomplished.

Plan Some Time Just for Fun

Recreational time helps keep you mentally and physically healthy. But get your work done first. Free time feels freer when you don't have unfinished business.

Be Flexible

Things change. Your schedule isn't carved in stone. Give yourself room to adapt to new circumstances and take advantage of new opportunities.

Don't Overschedule Yourself

Some people overeat; others overschedule themselves. If you have too much to do, you need to go on a schedule diet. Review your activities. Which ones can you live without?

Plan Time to Get Organized

Getting organized takes getting used to. Plan a few minutes each day to work on your schedules and clean up your learning environment. Think about what you need to do and how you're going to do it. You'll save hours of time you might have wasted.

Find and Use Little Chunks of Time

Waiting for a bus, in between classes, just before your favorite TV show—these are all little chunks of time you can put to good use. Choose something small, get it done, and get it out of the way.

Don't Procrastinate

Most people procrastinate for a reason. Maybe the task they're facing is too hard. Maybe it's too stressful. Whatever the cause, procrastination can become a bad habit. The best cure is to simply dig in and do the job. If you really, truly can't get started, talk it over with a friend, a teacher, or another trusted adult.

Cathy's Tip for Early-Morning Studying

Cathy likes to get up early in the morning to study and do final reviews for tests. She knows that this doesn't work for everyone, but she feels at her best in the morning hours—fresh and alert. Cathy has recognized that she's a morning person. She organizes her time around that fact.

How to → Keep Track of Daily Assignments

Some teachers write assignments on the board. Some give handouts that list the assignments for a week or a month. Some record assignments on a telephone service, and students can dial in to get the message. Some might even post assignments at the school's or class's Web site.

But other teachers just call out assignments at the end of class, and you can't hear because the bell is ringing and other kids are packing up their books and your friends are reminding you about basketball practice and someone knocked your notebooks on the floor.

No matter what, *you are responsible for knowing about and completing your assignments.* Don't leave class until you understand an assignment, even if it means staying after for a few minutes. Write down *all* assignments. Don't count on your memory.

Assignment Sheets: Some teachers provide assignment sheets. If yours don't, page 101 has one you can copy and use. Use *one* assignment sheet for *all* of your classes. Slip it into the notebook you carry all the time. At the end of the day, use it like a shopping list to decide what you need to take home from your locker.

"To Do" Lists: A "to do" list is a great place to record assignments. Write down directions as well as due dates. Having a list of things to do is a good thing. Listing tasks and, even better, crossing them off gives a real sense of accomplishment.

Some people prefer categorized "to do" lists. The categorized format can help you plan activities in blocks and manage your time every day. A blank planning sheet can be found on page 102. You can make copies of the planning worksheet and keep them in a three-ring binder.

Handheld Computer: A handheld computer or PDA (Personal Digital Assistant) can be used to keep track of appointments, things to do, addresses, phone numbers, and other data. Data on the handheld computer can by transferred or "synchronized" with software on your computer at home. The obvious downside of taking a handheld computer to class is the risk that it will be broken, lost, or stolen . . . big risks for such expensive technology.

What Good Does Homework Do?

Most teachers don't give homework just to make your life miserable. Homework can be good for you because . . .

. . . it encourages you to practice skills you haven't fully learned yet,

. . . it gives you opportunities to review skills you might forget,

. . . it enriches your store of general knowledge, adding to what you already know and helping you to learn new things,

. . . it teaches you responsibility,

. . . it helps you learn time-management skills,

. . . it gives you time to be creative and expand your learning, and

. . . it allows for tasks that are too time-consuming to finish during regular school hours.

13

Terrible Excuses
for Not Turning In Your Homework on Time

1. "I left it in my pocket and my mom put my jeans in the wash." **2.** "I left it on the bus (on my bed, in my locker . . .)." **3.** "The dog (cat, rat, computer) ate it." **4.** "I didn't do it because I had choir practice." **5.** "I didn't do it because I left my books at school." **6.** "I didn't do it because my mom (dad, sister, brother, aunt, grandfather) forgot to remind me." **7.** "I didn't do it because I had to finish an assignment for another class." **8.** "You didn't tell us to do it." **9.** "I didn't hear you tell us to do it." **10.** "I wasn't listening." **11.** "It was due today?" **12.** "What homework?" **13.** (Silence)

How to ▶ Handle Homework Problems

Problem: "I have a lot of other things to do, so I don't have time for homework."

SOLUTION: Homework is not an option. Eliminate some of your other activities.

Problem: "I let my homework go until the last minute."

SOLUTION: Use assignment sheets. See page 101.

Problem: "I don't pay attention to how important homework is for my grade. Then it's too late."

SOLUTION: Listen to your teachers when they tell you what counts in their classes. Most will base at least part of your grade on your homework.

Problem: "I forget to take my books home, or I forget to bring my homework to class."

SOLUTION: See page 8 for tips on how to keep your materials organized in your locker and at home.

Problem: "I forget the instructions. Sometimes I don't understand them in the first place."

SOLUTION: Write down all assignments and directions. If there's something you don't understand, ask the teacher or a friend to explain.

Problem: "I spend a lot of time on homework, but I still can't get it all done."

SOLUTION: Are distractions keeping you from working (TV, phone calls, noise, interruptions)? If distractions aren't the problem, talk to your teachers. See if they have any suggestions.

Problem: "All of my teachers assign homework on the same day. Then they give tests on the same day. I can't keep up!"

SOLUTION: Use assignment sheets to organize the assignments you know about in advance. Ask your teachers if they can give you longer lead times on assignments. If your work still piles up, talk to your teachers. See if they're willing to compare their schedules and give assignments and tests on different days. If this doesn't work, take your problem to the student council or the school counselor.

What to Do If You Get Behind

Everyone gets behind in their homework sometimes. This can happen for a lot of reasons. People get sick, overschedule themselves, have personal problems, get disorganized—but mainly, people aren't perfect.

The key to getting out of the hole is not to fall too far in. As soon as you feel yourself slipping, do something! Use assignment sheets (see page 101) to organize your work. Update your planning calendar or assignment notebook. Stick to your study schedule, and add time for makeup work.

If you still can't catch up, make an appointment to talk to your teachers. Consider inviting your parents, too. You'll probably surprise everybody. But if you take the initiative, grown-ups will know that you're serious about straightening out the mess you're in.

Tips for Talking to Teachers

- Think about what you want to say *before* you go into your meeting. Make notes and bring them along.

- Choose your words carefully. Instead of saying, "I'm behind because *you* give too much homework," you might say, "I'm behind on my schoolwork, and I want to catch up. Do you have any suggestions?"

- Don't expect the teacher to have all the answers. Come prepared with your own ideas.

- Be polite and respectful. Remember that the purpose of your meeting is conversation, not confrontation.

- Focus on what you need, not on what you think the teacher is doing wrong. The more the teacher learns about you, the more he or she can help. If a teacher feels defensive, it's less likely he or she will want to help.

- Don't forget to listen.

- Bring your sense of humor. Not the joke-telling kind, but the kind that lets you laugh at yourself and your own mistakes.

- If your meeting isn't successful, get help from another adult. Talk to the school counselor or another teacher you know and trust. Pick someone you think is likely to want to help you. Then try again.

"When in doubt, tell the truth."
—MARK TWAIN

Know When to Ask for Help

Successful people in the world of work (doctors, business professionals, teachers) know when to ask for help. Successful students also know when to ask for help. Developing good help-seeking strategies can benefit you in school and in later life. You can get help from a variety of sources:

teachers

family members

friends

neighbors

volunteer tutors at your school or in an after-school program

homework hotlines— online and on the phone

paid tutors

librarians

Here are some tips for successful help-seeking:

- Don't be afraid to ask for help—even experts need help sometimes.

- Ask for help early—don't wait until the last minute.

- Ask your teacher when is the best time for asking clarifying questions: before, during, or after class?

- If you have a tutor or another person who's willing to help, be prepared for the help session. Bring a list of questions, and come with all the necessary books and assignments you'll need for the session.

- Be willing to give help to others—sometimes you'll be the expert and can share your knowledge and skills with others.

Homework Help Online

Need some homework help in a jiffy? Try getting help using the Internet. Homework-help pages are available to provide information and support in a wide variety of subject areas. Use a search engine to help you find some of the many sites available. Here's a sample:

About Homework/Study Tips
www.homeworkhelp.about.com

This Web page includes links to over 700 sites to provide you with the help you need. It also has live chat rooms where a knowledgeable instructor can help answer your homework questions.

B.J. Pinchbeck's Homework Helper
school.discovery.com/homeworkhelp/bjpinchbeck

Put together by a father and son, this Web site, which gets over 10,000 visitors a day, provides more than 600 links that correspond with common homework problems.

Encarta Homework
encarta.msn.com/encnet/departments/homework

This site provides an excellent homework Web directory. In addition, the site provides specific suggestions for test preparation, writing reports, how to improve your writing, and other helpful homework tips.

Fact Monster™ from Information Please®
www.factmonster.com

The Fact Monster site is unique in combining essential reference materials, fun facts and features, and individualized homework help for kids. Useful for parents and educators as well as kids, it offers access to the full range of Information Please almanacs.

Jen and Alex's Homework and Reference Page
www.laser-imprints.com/homework.htm

This site is a fantastic collection of links that can provide useful information, organized by subject area (arts, literature, science, social studies, etc.).

RefDesk.com
www.refdesk.com

Here is a great research tool for finding information on nearly every imaginable topic. From daily news to currency converters, this site is a virtual library of facts and figures.

How to ➤ Keep Track of Long-Range Assignments

Many homework assignments can be completed in one night. Other assignments are more complicated and take a longer time to complete. Art and science fair projects, social studies displays, and research papers are examples of long-range projects. Special projects can be nightmares! They can also lead to last-minute panics and desperate acts, such as attempting to write a 20-page research paper in a single night.

There's a guaranteed way to avoid the hassle and actually enjoy your long-range assignments. It's called P-L-A-N-N-I-N-G.

This planning is necessary if you're going to complete the project on time and avoid a last minute rush. As soon as you hear about a long-range assignment, make a project plan. Follow this checklist (or copy and use the form on pages 103–104):

- ✔ Decide on a project theme.
- ✔ Have the theme approved by your teacher.
- ✔ Make a list of things you need to do to complete your project. Rank them in the order they need to be done.
- ✔ Decide if you'll need help from your parents or other adults. Ask if and when they can help you. Be clear about what you want them to do.
- ✔ Set deadlines for finishing each part of your project. Write the dates in your assignment notebook or planning calendar.
- ✔ Make a list of materials you'll need. Estimate how much they'll cost.
- ✔ Send away for resource materials.
- ✔ Contact community resources.
- ✔ Visit the library.
- ✔ Check the Internet for related Web sites.
- ✔ Complete your project on schedule.

Jerry's Tips for Completing Long-Range Projects

My husband, Jerry, has always had a knack for planning and completing long-range projects. Most recently, Jerry reached a lifelong goal to paddle a canoe down the entire Mississippi River. He started at the source of the river in Lake Itasca, Minnesota, and finished in New Orleans, Louisiana.

According to Jerry, he uses the same basic strategies to plan any long-range project. As Jerry puts it, "Learning how to plan and complete a long-range project is a skill that's important in all aspects of life." Here are Jerry's tips for planning and completing long-range projects:

- Start planning as soon as an assignment is given—don't waste a day.
- Break the big project down into smaller parts—inch by inch anything is a cinch!
- Schedule a certain amount of time every day to work on your project—a minimum of five days a week.
- If you miss a day—don't miss a second day. Get right back to your project.
- Talk about your project with your friends, parents, teachers—anyone you can. Soon people will start looking for resources to help you out.
- Plan time to plan. Plan your work and work your plan.
- Think about the information you'll need to complete your task and then use multiple resources: the library, the Internet, book stores, experts in the field.
- Think about the equipment you'll need to complete your task.
- Keep all your materials and designate a space for the project in one room. All paper-related materials can be put in a file drawer (work on the files a little every week to keep them organized). Keep bulky materials in containers in one section of the room.
- Have fun and be prepared to learn.

Plan to Succeed

Successful people don't become successful by accident or luck. They plan to succeed. They set goals and work to achieve them. They recognize problems that may get in their way and come up with solutions.

You can also plan to succeed. Start by filling out and using a goal-setting chart (see page 105). In two to four weeks, look back at your chart. Have your goals changed? Have you solved some of your problems? Have you had other successes? Add these to the Update section (see page 106). Then fill out a new goal-setting chart.

Keep doing this throughout the school year—every month or so. At the end of the year, you'll have a record of all your goals and successes.

P.S. It's nice to begin this goal-setting process at the start of a new school year. But you can do it anytime and get results.

The Checkpoint System: Six Steps to Success

Before takeoff, an airplane pilot goes through a series of checkpoints to make sure that everything is ready for a safe journey. Having your own checkpoints will help you succeed at school.

1 **At Home:** Before you leave the house, check to make sure you have everything you need for the day (backpack or bookbag, supplies, books, lunch, homework, signed notes, special projects, planning calendar or assignment notebook, good mood . . .).

2 **At Your Locker:** Before going to class, stop at your locker and check to see that you have everything you need.

3 **In Class:** Before leaving class, record your assignments. If you need to ask questions or clarify directions, do it *before* you leave the classroom. Make sure that you know the due date of every assignment.

4 **At Your Locker:** Before going home at the end of the day, check your assignment sheet. Get everything you need to complete your homework.

5 **At Home:** Check your daily schedule, then stick to it. Keep your commitment to study and do your homework at the same time each day, if at all possible.

6 **At Home:** Before going to bed for the night, put your backpack or bookbag, supplies, books, homework, signed notes, special projects, and anything else you'll need for the next day in one place, preferably the same place every night. This will make it easier to leave for school in the morning.

"Know when to listen and you will profit even from those who talk badly."

—PLUTARCH

Listen & Take Notes

LISTENING HABITS INVENTORY

What kind of listener are you? Find out by taking this Listening Habits Inventory.

You'll need a piece of paper and something to write with. Number the paper from 1–12. For each statement, give yourself 2 points if you *always* do it, 1 point if you *sometimes* do it, and 0 points if you *never* do it.

1. I'm in my seat and ready to listen soon after the bell rings.

2. I don't do other things while the teacher is talking.

3. I don't talk with friends while the teacher is talking.

4. I listen carefully to directions.

5. I ask questions when I don't understand directions or other information the teacher presents.

6. I take notes when the teacher presents a lot of information.

7. I know when the teacher is making an important point.

8. If I catch myself daydreaming, I try to get back on track.

9. I look at the teacher when she or he is talking.

10. I concentrate on what the teacher is saying.

11. If someone else is keeping me from listening, I ask that person to stop talking. If this doesn't work, I ask the teacher to help or change my seat.

12. I spend more time listening than talking in class.

Scoring: Add up your points.
16–24 points: You're a good listener! **12–15 points:** You need to be a better listener! **11 points or less:** Huh?

Listening
FACTS

Did you know that...

- most of the information and directions presented in class are given *orally* by the teacher?

- hearing is *not* the same as listening? Hearing simply means that sounds are coming into your ears, like waves pounding a shoreline. Listening means that you're actually *thinking* about the sounds and trying to *understand* and *remember* their meaning.

- it's very difficult to listen and do something else at the same time?

- you listen better when you look directly at the speaker?

- you listen better when you add personal meaning to what you hear? For example, if the teacher is talking about career awareness, think about the careers of some people you know.

- you listen better when you try to predict what the speaker will say next? For example, if the teacher says, "You're responsible for three experiments," expect to hear descriptions of all three even if the teacher doesn't say, "First . . . , second . . . , third . . . "

5
Reasons to Take Notes

Some people can remember everything they hear. The rest of us need to take notes! Here are five reasons why:

1. Your teacher probably covers information that isn't covered in the textbook. If you don't write it down, you won't have it when you need it.

2. Class notes are your best record of what happens during class, and your best source of material for test reviews.

3. Writing things down reinforces what you hear and helps you to remember.

4. Taking notes makes you a more active listener. You're less likely to doze off.

5. Note-taking skills are critical for success in high school and college. You may think you don't need them now, but you'll definitely need them later. Now is the time to learn.

Note-Taking Tips

Before Class:

- Read your assignment so you're ready to listen.

- Review your notes from the last class.

During Class:

- Write down the date and title of each lecture.

- Don't worry about punctuation or grammar.

- Use abbreviations for speed and efficiency.

- Don't write down every word the teacher says.

- Don't write down everything the teacher writes on the board.

- Underline, circle, or star anything the teacher repeats or emphasizes.

- Don't write more than one idea per line.

- Listen for digressions (times when the teacher gets off the subject). It's okay to take a mental break during these—but don't fall asleep.

- Write down any questions the teacher asks, since these are likely to appear on future tests.

- Don't cram your writing into a small space. Leave room to add more notes later.

- Put question marks by any points you don't understand. Check them later with the teacher.

After Class:

- Read your notes as soon as possible after class—ideally within 24 hours.

- Reorganize or type your notes if this will help you understand and remember them.

- Spell out any abbreviations you may not remember later.

- Highlight important points in your notes. This will help you find facts fast when you review for tests.

- Jot down any additional questions you may need to ask the teacher.

- If you're absent from class, get the notes from a friend.

Three Ways to Take Notes

There are many ways to take notes. Most good students develop a note-taking style that's comfortable and that works for them. If you haven't yet found the right style for you, try these:

1. Free-form

Write one idea per line and leave plenty of blank space. After class, you may want to rewrite, outline, or type your notes. Or use a colored highlighter to mark key concepts and ideas.

> 10/25
>
> Training for Knighthood
>
> only for males from noble families
> first step—page (7 yrs.)
> sent away from home
> learn religion, hunting, manners
> second step—squire (15/16 yrs.)
> learned skills to prepare for war
> also learned arts—music and poetry
> finally—knighthood! (21 yrs.)
> ceremony held in church
> sword blessed
> knight promised to be virtuous and valiant

2. The Cornell System

The Cornell note-taking system was invented by Dr. Walter Pauk at Cornell University. Many students from middle school through college have used it successfully. It involves five simple stages: *Record, Reduce, Recite, Reflect,* and *Review.* Think of these as the "five Rs."

Stage 1: Record
Divide your notebook page into two columns by drawing a vertical line. The narrow column (about one-third of the page) is the *recall column.* You leave it blank during the lecture. The wider column (about two-thirds of the page) is the *note-taking column.* Here's where you record your notes during the lecture.

Training for Knighthood

only for males from noble families
page (7 yrs.)
sent away from home
learn religion, hunting, and manners
squire (15/16 yrs.)
learned skills to prepare for war
learned arts—music and poetry
finally knighthood!
ceremony in church
sword blessed
knight promised to be virtuous and valiant

Stage 2: Reduce

As soon after class as possible (within 24 hours and certainly before your next class), reduce your notes to as few key words as possible. Write these in the *recall column*.

Training for Knighthood

	only for males from noble families
page	page (7 yrs.)
	sent away from home
	learn religion, hunting, and manners
squire	squire (15/16 yrs.)
	learned skills to prepare for war
	learned arts—music and poetry
Knighthood	finally knighthood!
	ceremony in church
	sword blessed
	knight promised to be virtuous and valiant

Stage 3: Recite

Cover the *note-taking column* with a blank piece of paper. Look at the key words in the *recall column*. Try to recite all the information you can't see. This self-service mini-test will help you prepare for the real thing.

Stage 4: Reflect

After reciting your notes, wait for a while. Then, without looking at your notes, think about the information they contain. Are there any big ideas you need to remember for a test? Do you have any unanswered questions about the information? Are there any really hard parts you need to spend more time on?

Stage 5: Review

Review your notes from time to time. If you do this on a regular basis, you'll be more than ready for any test that comes along. You may even want to schedule your reviews on a calendar.

3. Outline

If your teacher lectures from an outline, or if your teacher's lecture follows the textbook very closely, you may want to use a *formal* or an *informal* outline style for taking notes.

Use the teacher's organization to order your outline. Keep your notes brief. Don't try to write down every word your teacher says.

Formal outlines can be organized into several levels. Use as many of these as you need, and line up the different levels underneath each other. Don't start a new level unless you can break it down into at least two parts. In other words, don't start a level "1" unless you're fairly sure you'll also have a level "2."

Title of Lecture
I. Roman numerals for major headings
   A. Capital letters for subheadings
      1. Arabic numerals for important facts
         a. Lowercase letters for related facts and ideas

10/25

Training for Knighthood

I. Page
   A. About age 7
   B. Studied (away from home)
      1. Religion
      2. Hunting
      3. Manners

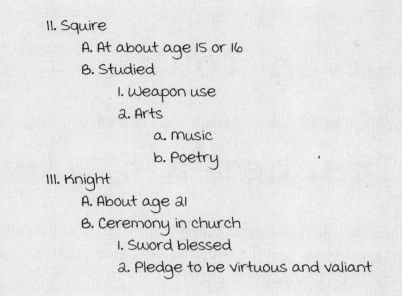

II. Squire
    A. At about age 15 or 16
    B. Studied
        1. Weapon use
        2. Arts
            a. Music
            b. Poetry
III. Knight
    A. About age 21
    B. Ceremony in church
        1. Sword blessed
        2. Pledge to be virtuous and valiant

Informal outlines are less structured. Number main facts and ideas, then line up related information using numbers, dashes, stars—whatever you choose.

10/25

Training for Knighthood

only for males from noble families
1. page (about age 7)
    boy sent away from home
    studied
        — religion
        — hunting
        — manners
2. Squire (about age 15 or 16)
    prepared for war
    learned
        — to use weapons
        — poetry, music, etc.
3. Knight (about age 21)
    ceremony in church
    sword blessed
    pledged to be virtuous and valiant

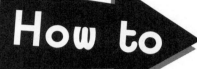

Match Your Notes to Your Teacher's Style

Some teachers follow the textbook, and some don't. Some write outlines on the board, and some don't. Some tell you everything, and some don't seem to tell you anything.

Obviously you can't treat every teacher (and class) the same. For maximum learning and best (test) results, adapt your note-taking style to your teacher's teaching style.

Read the following descriptions of "typical teachers." Think about what kind of notes you should take for each class. Then, read our suggestions.

▶ Mrs. Vaughn never uses a textbook. Class lectures *are* her class.

▶ Mr. Taylor never refers to the textbook in class. But he always tests on the textbook material.

▶ Ms. Rodriguez follows the textbook exactly.

▶ Mr. Masterson follows the textbook sometimes. At other times, he uses his own lecture notes.

For Mrs. Vaughn's class: Take lots of notes; don't rely on your memory alone. You'll be tested on what she says in class.

For Mr. Taylor's class: Take lots of notes and read your textbook carefully. (For tips on being a better reader, see pages 43–59.) Spend time merging the information from your class notes and textbook. How are they alike? How are they different? Is there conflicting information? Talk to the teacher if your book and his lectures don't agree.

For Ms. Rodriguez's class: Read the textbook chapter(s) before going to class. Take notes during class. Afterward, reread the textbook chapter(s).

For Mr. Masterson's class: Keep a complete set of class notes and read the textbook carefully. Spend time merging the information from both sources.

Note-Taking
INVENTORY

From time to time, it's smart to check the quality of your notes to see how you're doing. Then you'll know if you need to make any changes or improvements. Use this Note-Taking Inventory whenever you feel the need. Simply check it against that day's class notes.

You'll need a piece of paper and something to write with. Number the paper from 1–10. Give yourself one point for each item you find in your notes.

1. Date of lecture

2. Title of lecture

3. Writing neat enough for you to read (that's all that counts)

4. No more than one idea per line

5. Plenty of blank space to add extra ideas later

6. All main ideas brought up during class

7. All important details mentioned during class

8. All key terms and definitions given during class

9. Abbreviations used where necessary

10. No unnecessary words

Scoring: Add up your points.
9–10 points: You're a great note-taker!
7–8 points: You're a good note-taker.
5–6 points: You need to take better notes.
4 points or less: Make a note of this—practice, practice, practice!

If You Have Trouble Taking Notes

- Compare your notes with a friend's notes. (Pick a friend who you know is a good note-taker.) Add to your notes.

- Read the textbook chapter ahead of time. This will help you be a better listener (you'll already know some of what you hear) and note-taker.

- Talk to your teacher. Explain that you're trying, but it's hard to keep up. Ask the teacher to help you fill in the details.

- If you're really up a creek, ask the teacher if you can tape-record lectures and listen to them later. Then you can take notes at your own speed. But don't overuse this technique, or you could spend the rest of your life transcribing tapes.

- Keep practicing. Most middle-school students are just learning to take notes. Be patient; you'll get better at it.

How to Get the Most Out of Viewing

Sometimes your teacher lectures or leads a class discussion. Other class sessions might include additional activities. You might observe a science experiment demonstration or watch an educational video or TV program. You might even use a computer program or a Web site presented during class. If you're lucky, you might go on a field trip! Such special classroom activities are usually fun. So much fun that you might miss the point and forget what you need to know about the experience for the test.

Observation skills are becoming more important in classrooms throughout the country. When you're asked to participate in a viewing activity, the following strategy can help you get the most out of the experience. The strategy is called FOCUS.

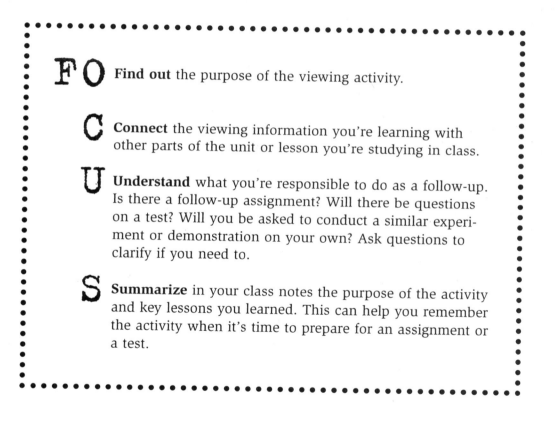

FO **Find out** the purpose of the viewing activity.

C **Connect** the viewing information you're learning with other parts of the unit or lesson you're studying in class.

U **Understand** what you're responsible to do as a follow-up. Is there a follow-up assignment? Will there be questions on a test? Will you be asked to conduct a similar experiment or demonstration on your own? Ask questions to clarify if you need to.

S **Summarize** in your class notes the purpose of the activity and key lessons you learned. This can help you remember the activity when it's time to prepare for an assignment or a test.

Speak UP

SAY SOMETHING!

Your grade in some classes may depend, at least partly, on your participation in class discussions. So don't just sit there—say something!

Some students honestly don't know what to say. Others are afraid of saying the wrong thing. Some students fear that if they speak up, others will brand them "know-it-alls" or "teacher's pets."

If you're worried about any of these issues, start by speaking up in class only some of the time. You may find that others will join in. Once you experience some success, you'll be more comfortable increasing your own level of participation.

Almost anyone can add something meaningful to class discussions. The secret lies in this basic Boy Scout rule: *Be prepared.* If you keep up with your assignments and pay attention to what others are saying, you can make a contribution, too.

How to ➤ Learn New Words

A bigger vocabulary can help you express your thoughts and feelings more clearly. It can make what you say sound more interesting. It can also improve your performance on tests and make you a better reader.

We learn new words naturally all the time by listening to our parents, friends, teachers, and TV. With a little effort and a lot of curiosity, you can give your natural learning tendency a push in the right direction.

✔ Develop word radar. Become aware of new words as you read and hear them.

✔ Make an effort to remember new words. Keep a list in your notebook, or start a word box with index cards. Write a new word on the front of each card and the definition on the back. Store your cards alphabetically in a file box. Watch your collection grow.

✔ If you come across a new word in a textbook you can't write in, jot down the word on a removable self-stick note and stick it in the book.

✔ Try to figure out the meanings of new words from their context—the familiar words and phrases that surround them. If you find a word you can't understand, look it up in the dictionary.

✔ Use a "word-a-day" calendar in your home study center. Learn each day's new word. Or subscribe to an online "word-a-day" service. Merriam-Webster offers a Word of the Day. To subscribe, check out the Web site at *www.m-w.com*.

✔ Use a thesaurus. The root meaning of the word "thesaurus" is "treasury." Think of your thesaurus as a treasury of new words, waiting to be discovered by you.

✔ Use your head. When someone around you says a new word, ask what it means.

✔ Be a word detective. Let your curiosity inspire you to learn more about a word than its meaning. Check its pronunciation. Find out where it came from. Examine its roots and track down related words.

✔ Put on your Sherlock Holmes hat and head for the *Oxford English Dictionary*, called the "OED" for short. Most libraries carry this important reference work. It traces words back through time to their earliest uses, showing how spellings and meanings have changed.

✔ Become an *etymologist*—a student of words.

How Diana Lia Learns New Words

Diana Lia is a top-notch student who enjoys learning new vocabulary words. Here's how she does it:

1. She makes a list of the new words she wants to learn with their definitions.

2. She covers the definitions to see if she can remember them.

3. She makes a new list of the words and definitions she didn't get right the first time.

4. She tests herself on this list.

5. She makes *another,* shorter list . . . and on and on until she masters all of the words and definitions.

6. Finally, Diana Lia goes back to her original list an hour or two later. She tests herself on all the words and definitions to find out if she has *really* learned them. If necessary, she goes through her listing-and-testing process again.

Class Discussion Tips

Do . . .

- ask legitimate questions based on reading you've done ahead of time.

- ask legitimate questions about what others say in class.

- listen carefully to what others have to say.

- add any information you may have to a point someone else makes.

- share personal experiences related to the topic when this will enhance the discussion.

- make statements or ask questions showing that you came to class prepared.

- give yourself three to five seconds of thinking time before answering a question. Your answers will be more accurate and interesting.

- be kind when you disagree with what somebody else says.

Don't . . .

- make comments that take up too much class time.

- make comments just to hear yourself talk.

- make a habit of going off the subject.

- interrupt others.

- get into arguments.

"Be curious always! For knowledge will not acquire you: you must acquire it."

—Sudie Back

How to ▶ Give Class Presentations

Most people need a great deal of instruction and practice to become skilled public speakers. That's why most high schools and colleges offer courses in public speaking.

Even if you've never taken such a course, you may be required to speak in front of your class. This can be scary, especially without training. You may get stage fright or butterflies in your stomach. Join the crowd! Many experienced speakers report the same symptoms.

Keep in mind that your teacher doesn't expect you to perform like a trained speaker. Class presentations in middle school are mainly warm-up exercises for the more formal presentations you'll give in high school and college. So don't worry about being perfect. Just do the best you can.

Presentation Preparations

- Organize your presentation in the same way you would organize a written paper. Think about your audience, topic, purpose, and format. For tips on preparing a written paper, see pages 62–66.

- Brainstorm power-packed opening and closing statements. These are the parts of your speech that your listeners will remember most.

- Time yourself. Stick to the time limit your teacher specifies.

- Include examples, stories, jokes, and interesting facts.

- Use visuals such as charts, graphs, and overheads, but be sure to practice using them ahead of time so you don't fumble during your presentation.

- Add computer technology to your presentations by learning how to use software such as Power Point.

- If you don't feel comfortable giving your presentation from memory, ask if it's okay to write it out and read it aloud. Or try speaking from an outline on index cards.

- Appearances count. Dress appropriately the day of your presentation.

Presentation Practice Tips

If you'll be going solo . . .

- Think about which teachers you like to listen to, and which ones you don't. Try to figure out what they do that makes you feel this way. Use your observations to plan your own presentation.

- Practice giving your speech in front of a mirror. This will help you see what your audience will be seeing.

- Practice saying your speech into an audio or video recorder. Afterward, listen and/or watch. Are you going too fast? Are you mumbling? Are you saying words like "um" or "like" too much? Do you sound excited? Notice areas that need improving.

If you'll be giving your report with a group . . .

- Make sure that *each* group member is aware of his or her responsibilities. Don't just assume that Marcus will do the summary at the end. Write down *all* of the report-related group responsibilities and assign them to individual group members.

- Practice with your group members using time limits. Afterward, share suggestions and practice again.

- Practice with visuals and props. For example, you may want one group member to hold up a poster during the presentation. Rehearse this in advance so you don't waste valuable presentation time sorting out who's supposed to do what when.

"It is better to ask some of the questions than know all the answers."

—James Thurber

How to ➤ Do Interviews

You can dress up class projects with facts, anecdotes, and information gathered during interviews with experts on the subject.

Interviews can also help you get excited about your project. It's hard to stay bored when you're talking to someone who has made your topic her or his life's work.

For example, if you're studying economics, you may want to interview a family friend who's a banker. If you're studying ecology, try interviewing a neighbor who works with the city water department.

Doing an interview involves more than just asking questions. Follow these guidelines for a successful experience everyone can enjoy.

Before the interview

- Find someone who has expertise in your subject area.
- Write or call to make an appointment for the interview. Be sure to:
  - schedule enough time.
  - tell your expert why you want to do the interview.
  - tell your expert what (if anything) he or she needs to do to prepare for the interview.
  - get permission to audiotape or videotape the interview.
  - thank your expert in advance for agreeing to do the interview.
- Before the interview, confirm the appointment date, time, and place.

Prepare your questions ahead of time. Include the specific questions you want to ask, plus a few general warm-up questions about the subject. If this is your first interview, ask your teacher to review your list of questions.

During the interview

- Arrive on time or a little bit early.
- Dress appropriately.
- Thank your expert for agreeing to do the interview.
- Act interested and enthusiastic.

- Start the interview with a few general questions.

- Follow up with more detailed questions.

- Listen carefully.

- Avoid debating with your expert. This isn't the time to argue or make the expert see your point of view.

- Stay within the time limit agreed upon in advance. Go over only if your expert says it's okay.

- Thank your expert again at the end of the interview.

- Offer to show your expert a copy of your interview summary before you turn it in to your teacher. This will allow your expert to correct any misunderstandings.

After the interview

- Write up your summary as soon as possible.

- Stick to the facts without inserting your personal feelings or opinions.

- Write your expert a thank-you note.

Contact Experts Through Email

You may decide (or your teacher may suggest) to contact an expert by email to get information for a report, a project, or an assignment. With email, you can contact people that might have been inaccessible before, such as professors from around the globe, scientists at NASA, or your favorite athlete. When asking an expert for information, there are several things to keep in mind:

- Your expert is probably a busy person. Keep your message short, but clear.

- In your request, explain the project you're working on and how interviewing this person would be helpful.

- If you're asking for information, allow ample time for your expert to respond, don't ask at the last minute—even with email.

- Don't expect that the expert will look up information for you or mail information to you. Keep your request modest.

- Ask permission to quote your expert's email response.

- Make certain that you send a thank-you response in a timely manner.

To learn more about email etiquette, check out the following Web site: *iwillfollow.com/emailetiquette.html*.

BECOME A BETTER READER

WHY YOU NEED TO READ

You already know that you need to read for school. But that's not the only reason. You'll be reading for the rest of your life. Almost everything you'll ever do— get a job, drive a car, shop, prepare a meal, pay a bill, plan a vacation, figure your taxes, rent a video, raise kids—requires reading skills.

Try to think of something that requires *no reading at all.* Video games? (What about the instructions and strategy magazines?) Sports? (What about the ads for the latest basketball shoes or the stats on your baseball cards?) TV? (You won't know when your program is on if you don't read the TV guide.) Music? (How will you find your way through the CD bins at the store or read the lyrics to your favorite songs?) The ability to read is your ticket to information. It makes your life richer. It helps you be a better writer. It satisfies your curiosity and opens your mind. It expands your world and your imagination. It enables you to learn almost anything. It makes you a more interesting person. For more about reading, read on.

How to ⮕ Choose What to Read

Have you been to a bookstore lately? Bookstores today are lively, colorful, exciting places that offer thousands of choices. When people say, "I don't read because it's boring," it's often because they haven't found the *right book*.

How can you find the right book? Forget about the school projects, book reports, and teacher-pleasing reading. We're talking about the right book for *you*.

- Start with your interests. Do you like rock music, computer programming, hairstyles, rubber rafting? There are plenty of books on all of these topics.

- No right book yet? Move on to your needs. Do you need to learn how to play golf, redecorate your room, or research Colorado for your family vacation? You'll find tons of books on any and all of these.

- No right book yet? Think about your favorite movie or TV show. You'll find novels based on movies, biographies of stars, books about how television shows and movies are made, and much more.

- No right book yet? Try the Internet. Explore sites of interest to you—often they have recommended reading lists. You can also find book reviews and book lists at Web sites such as Booklist (*www.ala.org/booklist/index.html*) and The Book Bag (*www.teenreads.com*).

- No right book yet? Visit an online bookstore to find out about interesting books.

- Still no right book? Talk to your friends, an adult you share interests with, or your local librarian. They'll all have suggestions to pass on to you.

> "Reading makes immigrants of us all. It takes us away from home, but more important, it finds homes for us everywhere."
>
> —HAZEL ROCHMAN

How to Take Charge of Your Reading

Teachers can test your understanding of your textbook reading. But their tests only estimate whether you truly understand what you read.

You're the best judge of your own understanding. That's why you need to take charge of your reading. Follow these four steps:

1. Determine the level of difficulty of what you're reading.
2. Develop a plan for reading.
3. Become aware of when you do and don't understand what you read.
4. Know what to do when you don't understand what you read.

→ Step 1: Determine the level of difficulty of what you're reading

You've just turned to today's reading assignment. It's wall-to-wall words, no pictures, and the type is microscopic! Don't flip your lid. Instead, use FLIP to find out how hard your assignment really is. FLIP has four categories you complete by answering four questions.

F = Friendliness

Question: "How friendly is my reading assignment?"
How to decide: A text is friendly if it has lots of headings, subheadings, words in boldface type, and so on. It's unfriendly if it has few or none of these helpful features.

L = Language

Question: "How difficult is the language in my reading assignment?"
How to decide: Choose three paragraphs from different parts of your assignment. Read each paragraph out loud. Are the paragraphs filled with few new words and short, easy sentences? Or do they contain many new words and long, complicated sentences?

I = Interest

Question: "How interesting is my reading assignment?"
How to decide: Skim your assignment. (To learn about skimming, see page 49.) If you're interested in the subject, it'll probably seem easy to read. If you're not, it'll probably seem harder to read and take longer.

P = Prior knowledge

Question: "What do I already know about the material covered in my reading assignment?"
How to decide: If you already know a lot about a topic, reading about it will be easy. You'll just be reviewing what you already know, and maybe picking up a few new pieces of information. But if a topic is brand new to you, reading about it will probably be more difficult.

Pages 107–108 contain a FLIP Chart you can copy and use to rate your reading assignments. Notice that there are no "right" or "wrong" answers—just your own judgments. Plus, you're not trying to figure out what someone else thinks is easy or difficult. You get to decide for yourself.

When you're through FLIP-ing, add up your ratings and interpret your score. What does it tell you about your assignment? Is the reading level "comfortable," "somewhat comfortable," or "uncomfortable" for you?

Think of FLIP as a set of mental training wheels. Soon you'll be able to figure out an assignment's level of difficulty without FLIP-ing.

→ Step 2: Develop a plan for reading

Take-charge readers figure out their task and make a plan for accomplishing it. Your reading plan should include these three parts (see page 109 for a FLIP Chart Follow-Up that you can copy and use for your reading plan):

Set a purpose for your reading

What's your reason for reading a particular assignment? The obvious response is, "Because I have to." But try to be more specific. For example:

- for personal pleasure (because *I* want to)
- to prepare for class discussions
- to answer written questions for class assignments or homework
- to prepare for a test

Can you think of more? Circle or mark your purpose on the FLIP Chart Follow-Up.

Determine your reading rate

Is it okay to race through your reading assignment? Or should you stop on every word? That depends on your purpose for reading and how difficult your assignment is. Circle your reading rate on the FLIP Chart Follow-Up.

If your overall rating is . . .	and your purpose for reading is . . .	then your reading rate should be . . .
comfortable	personal enjoyment	RAPID
somewhat comfortable	preparing for a test or for class discussions	MEDIUM
uncomfortable	preparing for a test or for class discussions	SLOW

Budget your reading/study time

Many students open their books at the start of a study session and stop reading when they're tired. But there's a better way. "Chunk" the chapter—divide it into small study units. Read and study one chunk, take a break, then move on to the next chunk.

If you're reading a short assignment at a comfortable level, you may be able to finish it in one sitting. But if your assignment is long and/or uncomfortable, chunk it. Record your reading chunks on the FLIP Chart Follow-Up. Estimate how long it'll take you to read each chunk. Fill in your total estimated reading time.

→ Step 3: Become aware of when you do and don't understand what you read

You reach the end of a paragraph or page in your book, and suddenly you realize that you didn't understand a word. You don't remember a thing. You've been in the Reading Twilight Zone.

It happens to everybody. But problems come up when it happens all the time and you don't know it—or you don't do anything about it.

You can become aware of when you understand what you read. This is called developing *comprehension awareness.*

Think in terms of "clicks" in your brain. If it "clicks," then you understand it. When something "clunks," it's like a loose part on a car. You need to pull over and take a look under the hood.

Right after you finish reading a paragraph or page, think "click" or "clunk." If it's a "click," keep on reading. If it's a "clunk," try one of these reading repairs:

- Slow down. Change your reading rate.

- Keep reading anyway. A clue to help you understand may be coming up.

- Reread the paragraph or page.

- Use charts, graphs, tables, pictures, and other visuals to help you out. If there aren't any in the text, create your own.

- If you "clunked" on a new vocabulary word, look it up in the glossary or your dictionary.

- Go to another source. For example, maybe you're reading about photosynthesis in your science textbook, and it's too difficult. An encyclopedia article on the same subject might be easier to read. Skim that first, then return to your science textbook.

- Ask a friend, teacher, or parent for help. Getting help when you need it is an important part of being a take-charge reader.

"Books were my pass to personal freedom. I learned to read at age three, and soon discovered there was a whole world to conquer that went beyond our farm in Mississippi."

—OPRAH WINFREY

Take-Charge Reading Summary

Step 1: FLIP to determine the level of difficulty

   F = Friendliness

   L = Language

   I = Interest

   P = Prior knowledge

Step 2: Reading plan

   1. Your purpose

   2. Your reading rate (purpose + difficulty)

   3. Your reading time budget (chunk & estimate)

Step 3: Comprehension awareness

   "Clicks" and "clunks"

Step 4: Reading repairs

   ✔ Slow down

   ✔ Keep reading

   ✔ Reread

   ✔ Use visuals

   ✔ Look it up

   ✔ Try another source

   ✔ Ask for help

How to ➤ Be a Speedier Reader

Would you like to be able to read faster? Most people would. Speedier reading can reduce study time, boost test performance, and enable you to enjoy more novels and stories.

But it doesn't help to read faster if you don't remember what you read. The trick is to speed up your reading without losing comprehension. You do this by becoming a flexible reader, breaking bad reading habits, and practicing.

Get Flexible

You can learn to vary your reading rate, depending on what you're reading and why you're reading it. Here are four different rates to try (WPM = words per minute). *Tip:* This page has 302 words on it.

1. **Careful, analytical reading (50–300 WPM).** This is the rate to use for textbook material—stuff you'll be tested on later.

2. **Rapid reading (300–600 WPM).** If the material is easy for you, if you already know a lot about the subject, and if you're not going to be tested on it, go ahead and read quickly. You may even want to skip some parts. This is the rate to use for magazine articles, newspapers, or books you're reading for pleasure.

3. **Skimming (up to 1,500 WPM).** Preview a chapter, zip through a newspaper article, or race through a magazine piece using this reading rate. Skimming works best when you don't know what you're looking for and you're reading unfamiliar material. Your eyes may stop on a word here or there, or a paragraph that's especially interesting to you.

4. **Scanning (up to 3,000 WPM).** Use this supersonic rate to find a name in a telephone book, a word in a dictionary, a movie in the TV guide, or the answer to a textbook question after you've already read the chapter.

Continues on next page))

Break Bad Habits

- Do you point your finger at every word you read? Do you move your lips? These habits can slow you down. Instead of pointing at every word, hold a card under every line as you read it. This is a crutch, but it can help you break the pointing habit. (Later you can work on breaking the card habit—but by then you'll probably be reading faster.) Instead of moving your lips for everything you read, try to stop doing it for easy reading. This will be a positive step toward stopping altogether.

- Do you always go back and reread? Sometimes this can improve your comprehension. But you shouldn't have to read *everything* twice. If you reread too often, try being a more active reader. Highlight or take notes. Do *something!* This will help to focus your attention so you may not need to reread.

- Do you read every word on the page? Many slow readers do. It's much faster and more efficient to read in *word groups*. Don't let your eyes stop on every word. Instead, focus on three to four words at a time. For example, here's a sentence from the beginning of this section:

Speedier reading can reduce study time, boost test performance, and enable you to enjoy more novels and stories.

If this is how you would normally read it . . .

Speedier—reading—can—reduce—study—time, boost—test—performance, and—enable—you—to—enjoy—more—novels—and—stories.

. . . try mentally breaking it up into word groups . . .

Speedier reading / can reduce study time, / boost test performance, / and enable you / to enjoy more / novels and stories.

Notice that your eyes stop only six times instead of 18 times. Naturally, you'll read faster.

"When I was a kid in Philadelphia, I must have read every comic book ever published. I still read comic books in addition to contracts, novels, newspapers, screenplays, tax returns, and correspondence."

—BILL COSBY

Practice

- Try the four reading rates with different materials. Get a feel for each one. You'll soon discover which to use when.

- Mark off 100 words and time yourself when you read. Use a stopwatch, a watch with a second hand, or a kitchen timer. Start with books or articles that are easy for you. Try to remember what you read.

- Practice rapid reading on a newspaper article, magazine article, or short story. Write a two- or three-sentence summary.

- Skim a newspaper or magazine article. Write a one-sentence summary.

"When I look back, I am so impressed again with the life-giving power of literature. If I were a young person today, trying to gain a sense of myself in the world, I would do that again by reading, just as I did when I was young."

—MAYA ANGELOU

- Scan the telephone book for your name and your friends' names. Scan sports articles for high-action verbs.

- Read mysteries. Trying to solve "whodunits" will speed up your reading rate.

- Gradually move on to more difficult material. Try reading your textbook pages a little faster, but make sure that you can mentally summarize each page before you go on to the next.

- Try word-group reading a newspaper, where the columns are thin and the words group naturally.

How to ▶ Read Fiction

Literature includes everything that has ever been written, from comic books to classic novels. It's divided into two main categories: *fiction* and *nonfiction* (*informational text*).

Fiction is writing that comes out of the author's imagination, even though it may be based on real experiences and placed in actual historical or geographical settings. Even biographies—narratives about real people—can be fictional, if they include made-up stories about their subjects' lives.

Reading fiction should be *fun*. Think of novels, short stories, myths, and tall tales as personal videos for your mind. You're free to imagine what the scenes and characters look like. You're not limited by someone else's ideas (most fiction doesn't have pictures).

From time to time, you may be required to read fiction in school. Some teachers provide outlines or guidelines describing what they expect you to look for. These may seem boring, but they're not *all* bad. They can prepare you to participate in class discussions and perform well on tests.

On pages 110–111, is a Guide for Story Reading you can copy and use. Fill out one the next time you read a work of fiction. See if it helps you to understand and remember more of what you read. It'll come in handy for reviews, too. Here are some basic steps:

Step 1: Get ready. Think about ways to get involved in the story. If the story is set in a place that's unfamiliar to you, get out a map or an encyclopedia, or check on the Internet to learn more about where the story takes place. If the story is set during a historical time that's unfamiliar to you, do a little background reading.

Step 2: Get set. After reading the first few pages or the first chapter, think about the main characters of the story. Do any of the main characters remind you of someone you know or a character on TV? If you were in the same situation as the main character, how would you react? What would you do?

Step 3: Go. Read the rest of the story or read the book chapter by chapter. Stop occasionally to summarize and think about your own personal reactions to what's happening.

Step 4: Cool down. Immediately after reading the story, think about how you're reacting to the story. What parts were most enjoyable? What parts were least enjoyable? How do you feel about what happened in the story? What would you do if you were one of the characters? Think about the author's style. What words, phrases, or images struck you most?

Step 5: Follow up. Respond to the story in some way. Write about it. Talk about it. Draw about it. See 50 Fantastic Ideas for Book Sharing on pages 112–113 for some ideas.

How to Read Informational Text

Much of the reading you do for school is to learn new information—new vocabulary and new ideas. Informational text is writing that's factual in nature. Textbooks, encyclopedias, newspapers, and many biographies and autobiographies are examples of informational text.

This can be very slow and tedious reading—especially if you need to prepare for a test. You can't treat a textbook chapter like a story or a magazine article. If you do, you'll miss too much. Your teacher might provide reading strategies and assignments to help you learn from informational text. If not, The Guide for Reading Informational Text, on pages 114–115, can guide you through the reading of many subject areas: science, social studies, mathematics, and more. Here are the basic steps:

Step 1: Preview

Look at the pictures, headings and subheadings, introduction, and any summaries. Think about what you already know about the topic. Then predict what you're going to learn about the topic.

Step 2: Action reading

Don't just look at the words, read in an active way. Break the assignment into sections. Read one section at a time. After reading each section, identify and fix any "clunks" (difficult or confusing words or ideas). Then, list two or three key ideas that you think might be on a test.

Step 3: Wrap up

Think about your whole reading assignment. List the most important ideas and new words that you've learned. Finally, predict five or six questions the teacher might ask on a test. Think about other ways to record what you've learned. Pages 54–55 provide five ways to record what you've learned from informational text.

"The greatest gift is the passion for reading. It is cheap, it consoles, it distracts, it excites, it gives you knowledge of the world and experience of a wide kind."

—ELIZABETH HARDWICK

Ways to Record What You've Learned from Informational Text

Some students can read a chapter once and ace a test. Others succeed by reading the chapter several times. But for most of us, reading isn't enough.

We need to *do something* while we read—something that reinforces our reading, helps us remember what we read, and gives us a way to review our reading later. We need to be *active readers*.

1. Outlining

Pages 28–29 lists suggestions for outlining lectures. These work just as well for outlining what you read. Use the author's organization to order your outline. Keep your notes brief; don't copy the whole chapter.

2. Note-taking

There are several great ways to take notes. Try free-form notes, as described on page 26, or the Cornell System, described on pages 26–28. Or:

- Create study flash cards with 3"x 5" index cards. Write a question or key word on the front of each card. Write the answer or definition on the back.

- Make study tapes. Record "teacher-like" questions as you read. Pause after each question and record the answer.

3. Semantic mapping

Semantic mapping gives you a verbal picture of a chapter. It illustrates how ideas are organized and related. If you have strong visual memory, this is an excellent way to learn information for tests—especially essay tests.

For example, here's a semantic map on the subject of whales:

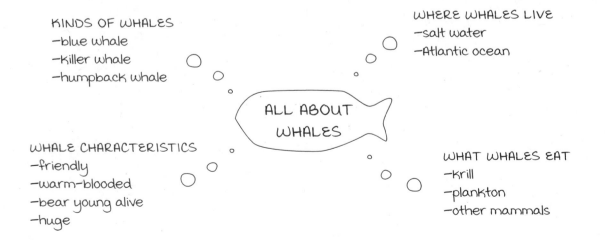

KINDS OF WHALES
—blue whale
—killer whale
—humpback whale

WHERE WHALES LIVE
—salt water
—Atlantic ocean

ALL ABOUT WHALES

WHALE CHARACTERISTICS
—friendly
—warm-blooded
—bear young alive
—huge

WHAT WHALES EAT
—krill
—plankton
—other mammals

It doesn't take much to turn these notes into an essay. For example, "There are many different kinds of whales, including the blue whale, killer whale, and humpback whale. Whales are warm-blooded, friendly, and huge! They bear their young alive, like other mammals . . . "

▶ How to Make a Semantic Map

1. Determine how the author organized the information in the chapter.
2. Write down a main idea and draw a shape around it.
3. Write down secondary ideas (no more than six or seven) and label them.
4. Add important details under each secondary idea. Be concise.
5. When your map is complete, talk yourself through it as if you were answering an essay question.

4. Summarizing

A summary is a *short* version of the original text that keeps the main message and follows an introduction-body-conclusion form.

▶ How to Write a Summary

1. Read the entire text.
2. Reread and underline important points.
3. Edit your underlined material.
4. Rewrite it in your own words.
5. Edit your version.
6. Check your version against the original.
7. Rewrite if necessary.

5. Annotating and highlighting

If your textbooks belong to you—if you don't turn them in at the end of the year—why not write in them? You'll have everything you need in one place (text, notes, questions), plus you'll conserve paper!

▶ How to Annotate and Highlight

1. Highlight new words and major points.
2. Bracket key passages.
3. Write new vocabulary words at the top of the page.
4. Star important facts.
5. Write numbers to order things in a series.
6. Put question marks by things you don't understand.
7. Summarize key paragraphs in margins.
8. Don't write more than the author! Don't overmark! If you find yourself highlighting *everything*, STOP. You're missing the whole point of highlighting.

How to ▶ Read the Classics

Classics are books that have stood the test of time. They've been read and loved for many years. Many have been made into comic books, cartoons, and movies because people never get tired of them.

The Adventures of Huckleberry Finn, Alice's Adventures in Wonderland, Oliver Twist, Go Tell It on the Mountain, Gulliver's Travels, Treasure Island, The Odyssey, The Little Prince, Rip Van Winkle— all are classics still worth reading.

You may decide to read them on your own. Or your teacher may decide for you. Either way, you'll face the same problems.

The language may be difficult. Sentences may be long. Vocabulary may be unfamiliar. The authors may use outdated expressions or figures of speech. References that made sense to people of that time period may not make sense to you.

Don't give up or get discouraged. Instead, try these tips:

- Don't read in bed. Reading the classics takes concentration.

- If you have a choice, start with something familiar. Have you seen the movie of *Treasure Island*? If yes, then you know the story. Now read the book.

- Read something about the author—for example, a brief encyclopedia article or find information on the Internet. Find out about his or her life and times. This will help you to understand the book a little better.

- Read in big chunks. Plan to spend an hour or so at a time reading. This will help you get into the book.

- Don't get frustrated by big words. Keep reading and try to get the big picture.

- Plan to reread the book in the future. It'll feel like visiting an old friend.

How to ▶ Follow Written Directions

Some people would rather do anything than follow written directions. This can get them into trouble at school.

If the directions for your social studies paper say, "Leave a two-inch margin at the bottom," and you leave a half-inch margin, you could lose points. If the directions for your math final say, "Circle the right answer," and you cross out the wrong answers, you could fail the test. It may not be fair, but it's a fact.

Here are written directions on how to follow written directions—can you follow them?

1. Read the whole set of directions slowly and carefully, out loud if you can, silently if you can't.

2. Underline, circle, or highlight the actions you'll need to take.

3. If the steps aren't already numbered, identify and number them yourself.

4. Try to imagine the steps in your mind before you actually start working.

5. When you have finished following the directions, retrace your steps. Make sure you've followed the directions *completely* and *correctly.*

How to ➤ Be a Critical Reader

Take-charge readers don't just read the text. They don't just comprehend what they read. They also make personal judgments about the author's message and ideas. They're *critical readers.*

Critical reading doesn't mean pointing out mistakes. Instead, it involves carefully examining what's being said, how it's being said, and who's saying it. It also involves comparing what you read to what you already know. Let's say you're an expert on Tyrannosaurus Rex. You've been reading about your favorite dinosaur since you were six years old. Now there's a new book out, *T. Rex: The Total Truth!* Because this is a subject you know a lot about, you'll be a good judge of whether the book is worth reading.

Try these critical reading techniques on a newspaper editorial or a controversial magazine article.

- Read the passage from beginning to end. Get a general idea of the author's message.

- Find evidence for the author's qualifications to write on this subject. Is she or he an expert? How do you know?

- If possible, find out who paid the author to write the passage. Does he or she work for a newspaper, a special-interest group, or a public relations firm? What difference does it make? You decide.

- What do you think was the author's reason or purpose for writing this passage?

- Identify three or four facts presented in the passage.

- Identify three or four opinions presented in the passage.

- Answer these questions for yourself: Does the author present both sides of an issue evenly? Or does she or he seem to be biased in one direction?

- Find any words the author used to get you emotionally involved with the issue.

- Decide whether you agree or disagree with the author. Be ready to explain the reasons for your decision.

Do You Know Propaganda When You See It?

Critical readers keep their eyes peeled for *propaganda*. Propaganda is writing that tries to persuade you to behave or believe a certain way. Look for examples of these propaganda techniques in advertisements, articles, and essays.

Testimonials
A famous person tells you how wonderful a product or idea is.
"I use it because . . . "
"I think this way because . . . "

Bandwagoning
The writer suggests that "most people" are in favor of a product or an idea—and you'll be "left out" if you don't agree.

Glittering Generalities
"New and improved!"
"More than before!"
"Extra-strength!"

"Plain Folks"
The writer uses informal, "at home" language.
"Like you, I believe that . . . "

Name-Calling
"The senator is racist because . . . "

Appeals to Prestige
"Dare to be different . . . "
"You're not the average person . . . "
"Only a very few people are privileged to . . . "

Emotional Language
"Mom, the flag, and apple pie . . . "
"Act quickly—before it's too late . . . "
"This little girl has never had a new toy . . . "
"You may already be a winner!"

Ten Ways to Sharpen Your Reading Skills

1. Set aside time each day for silent reading of things you're interested in. **2.** Read aloud to a younger child—a brother or sister, a neighbor, or a child you baby-sit. **3.** Be curious about new words. The more you learn, the better reader you'll be. **4.** Watch educational TV shows and videos. **5.** Be a take-charge reader. Determine the level of difficulty of each reading assignment. Develop a plan to complete it. **6.** Be aware of your level of understanding. Remember "clicks" and "clunks." Use reading repairs for "clunks." **7.** Be a flexible reader. Practice reading at different rates (slow and careful, rapid, skimming, and scanning). **8.** Visit the library often. Keep track of the books you read in a reading log. For each book, list the title and author, write a brief summary, then add your thoughts and opinions of the book. Note any problems you had while reading it and how you handled those problems. A spiral-bound notebook makes a fine reading log. **9.** Vary your reading. Don't limit it just to books or comic books. Try magazines, newspapers, catalogs, encyclopedias, dictionaries, etc. **10.** If you have trouble with your reading, tell your teachers. Tell your parents. Get help! This is part of being a take-charge reader.

Write Right

WRITING ONE STEP AT A TIME

Test answers and telephone messages. Notes and journals. Lists and letters. Papers and reports.

Like it or not, there are times when you have to write. Some middle schools require a lot of writing. Your writing load will only increase in high school and college, so it's best to learn the basics now.

Picture each writing assignment as a stairway. Each step you take will bring you closer to *getting it done.*

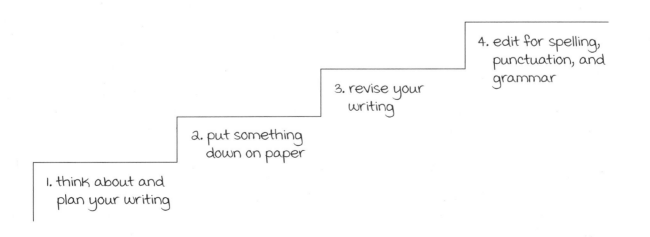

4. edit for spelling, punctuation, and grammar

3. revise your writing

2. put something down on paper

1. think about and plan your writing

How to ➤ Get Started

➤ Pick a Topic

1. What are you interested in learning more about?
2. Will you be able to find information about it?
3. Does your topic meet your teacher's requirements?

If you pick something you really want to learn about, you can probably make it fit your teacher's requirements. Your teacher may be more flexible if you show that you're genuinely committed to your topic.

Tip: Be specific. A paper on "Building an Igloo" is easier to write than "A History of World Architecture from the Beginning of Time to the Present Day."

➤ Choose a Purpose

Why are you writing? "My teacher made me do it" may be the truth, but it's not much to go on. Instead, try one of these:

- to explain
- to describe
- to tell a story
- to entertain
- to express my feelings
- to persuade

This gives your writing a sense of direction. If you know where you're going, you're more likely to get there.

➤ Find a Form

What form will your writing take—essay, story, poem, letter, report, or something else? Has your teacher given you specific instructions, or are you on your own? Ask if you're not sure.

Sometimes a story wants to turn into a poem. Sometimes an essay wants to turn into a story. Find out if you're free to be flexible. See Writing Ideas from A to Z (page 116) to give you ideas about different formats.

➤ Identify Your Audience

If you're writing a TV script for teenagers, you can use contractions and current slang. If you're writing a letter to the editor of your city newspaper, you must be more formal. Who are you writing to or for? Who is your reader? Your mom, your teacher, your friend, readers of the school newspaper? Keep your audience in mind while you write. This helps you choose the right words, sentence difficulty, and emphasis. It helps you decide on your style and tone.

What If You Hate to Write?

- Make sure that your topic is interesting to you—if not a lot, then at least a little. Keep an open mind. It may get more interesting, if you give it a chance.

- Don't procrastinate! You'll still have to write that paper even if you wait until the night before.

- If you have a computer (or access to a computer), use it to write your paper. See page 77 for reasons why.

- Set a goal and plan to reward yourself when you reach it. For example, "When I get my rough draft done, I'll watch my *King Kong Meets Godzilla* video."

- Try freewriting, described below.

- Try the Writer's Block Busters on page 73.

Writing Warm-Ups

Once you've picked your topic, use these strategies to get your brain in gear.

- Read something about your topic.

- Talk to other people about your topic.

- Brainstorm about your topic. Quickly write down as many ideas as you can that are related to your topic. Don't stop to think about whether your ideas are any good. Be creative—be crazy!

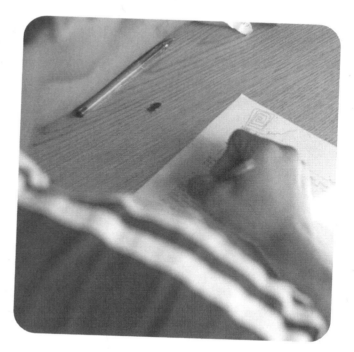

- Freewrite on paper about your topic. Give yourself five minutes to write anything that comes to mind. Don't let your pencil leave the paper. If you can't think of anything to write, then write, "I can't think of anything" over and over, until you can—and you will. Freewriting frees your mental powers.

- Freewrite on a computer. Darken the screen so you can't read or judge what you write. When you're finished, look at the results. You many find a brilliant idea or two.

How to ➤ Plan Your Writing

Some people can sit down and start writing. The rest of us have to plan what we want to say and how we want to say it.

1. Break down your assignment into small, manageable tasks. Plot these on an assignment sheet. Page 101 has one you can copy and use.

2. Predict how much *total* time your assignment will take. A good estimate is about an hour and a half per page (a 10-page paper = about 15 hours of work). Plan to finish a bit before your deadline, so you'll have extra time if you need it.

3. Be prepared to change your plan as needed. You may find that some tasks take longer than you thought, while others you finish sooner.

4. Put your ideas into some kind of rough organization. This will help you decide the order you'll present your information, what information doesn't fit, and where there are holes that need more information.

Diagrams

Diagrams can help you see how your information fits together. Your assignment may not need as much detail as these diagrams show, or it may need more.

Bubbles

Put a few ideas or facts in bubbles—one fact per bubble. Connect the bubbles in ways that make sense to you. Once you've filled a few bubbles, you'll get ideas for new ones to add.

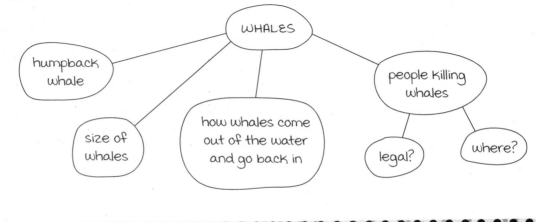

Flow Charts

A flow chart shows how ideas follow one another. Write your ideas or facts in boxes, join them with arrows, then look them over. Are there any information gaps that need filling in? Should you change the order of your ideas?

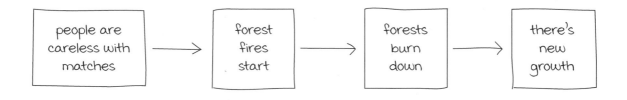

Cause and Effect

Cause-and-effect diagrams show how one event leads to another. Write your causes in circles, your effects in squares. Some ideas and facts can be both causes and effects. Draw as many cause-and-effect diagrams as you like, and combine them in the way that works for you.

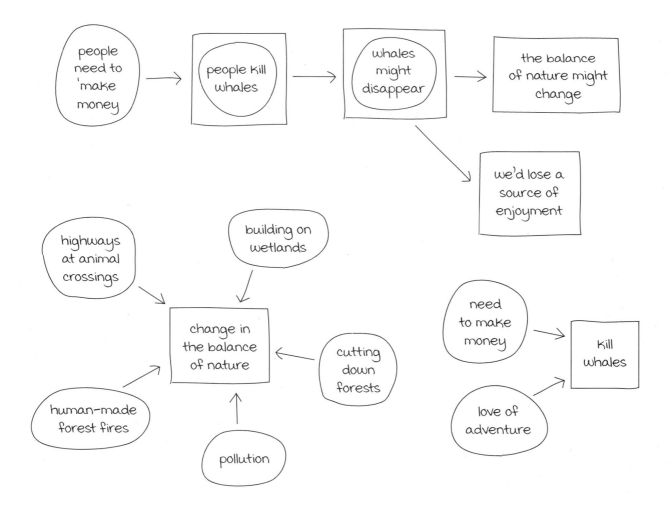

Compare and Contrast

How are two things the same? How are they different? A compare-and-contrast diagram can give you some answers. Look at the information in the section where the two circles meet. This might make a good starting point for your paper.

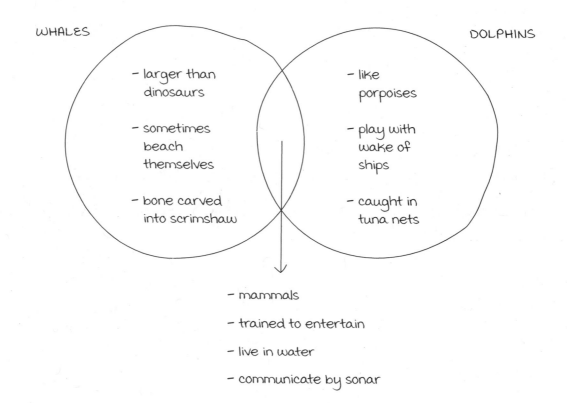

WHALES

- larger than dinosaurs

- sometimes beach themselves

- bone carved into scrimshaw

DOLPHINS

- like porpoises

- play with wake of ships

- caught in tuna nets

- mammals

- trained to entertain

- live in water

- communicate by sonar

Semantic Map

Pages 54–55 tell you how to use a semantic map to take charge of your reading. You can also use it to organize information for a writing assignment.

- Start with a topic.

- Think of possible categories about your topic.

- Find information to fit the categories. Be flexible—you may want to take out some categories and add others.

Outline

Pages 28–29 list suggestions for outlining lectures. Outlines work just as well for writing assignments. An outline is a tried-and-true way to organize information. The more detailed your outline is, the easier it will be to connect your facts and ideas and create paragraphs.

How to → Write a First Draft

You've picked your topic, purpose, and form. You've identified your audience. You've organized your facts and ideas. You can't put it off any longer. Start writing!

- Don't worry yet about spelling, punctuation, or "getting it right." Just get your ideas down on paper.

- For easier organizing and revising, use a computer.

- If you have trouble starting at the beginning, jump in anywhere. Write down a point you want to make. Then add sentences to introduce your point and sentences to support it. Before you know it, you'll have a complete paragraph.

- Double space or skip lines to leave room for revisions.

- Follow your writing plan for as long as it works. Remember that you can change it if and when you need to.

"The art of writing is the art of applying the seat of the pants to the seat of the chair."

—MARY HEATON VORSE

Marc's first draft

It all started when my mother, sister, & I went to an office supply store. I don't remember why, but I'm glad we did. While we were there the thought reacured to me (I say reacured because my parents & I had talked about it for years) that I needed new furnature (as in desk with hutch & book case). When I brought up the fact, my sister (of course, as usual) decided that she needed to get a desk to. That severly hurt my chances of getting the much needed furnature.

Luckly though, my mother explained to her that she

How to Revise and Edit Your Writing

Even professional writers need to revise and edit their writing. Nobody gets it 100-percent right the first time. A-OK is a five-part process for finding and fixing problems. If you can remember MOK, POK, SOK, WOK, and NOK, you can master this easy way to write right. Page 117 has an A-OK Checklist you can copy and use to revise and edit your own work. Have a family member or friend edit with you or after you. Another person may catch something you missed.

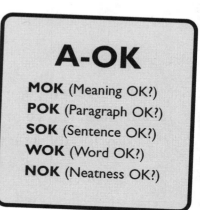

A-OK

MOK (Meaning OK?)
POK (Paragraph OK?)
SOK (Sentence OK?)
WOK (Word OK?)
NOK (Neatness OK?)

MOK (Meaning OK?)

Ask yourself these questions, one at a time. Read your paper out loud after each question or two. Mistakes are easier to catch when you 1) hear them, and 2) pay attention to only one thing at a time. Ignore any grammar or spelling errors for now; you can correct them later.

- "Does it make sense?"
- "Is it concise and to the point?"
- "Is it complete?"
- "Does it say what I really want it to say?"
- "Are my facts correct?"
- "Is there an introduction?"
- "Is there a conclusion?"

Repeat this process, reading your paper to a parent or a friend.

Marc's revisions

way befor a dissatisfied customer

could reach across the desk with a

knife,). That night when we got home

The one I liked best was a business desk.

until 2:00 A.M. Sunday. I also got a

roling chair from my Aunt and Uncle, who

came over for diner at abought 8:15 P.M. 30

(though (they said theyed be there by 8.
Consaquently diner got cold. (that Saturday
and stayed up drinking coffee.
After helping finish up the bookshelf thay
with my parents from 2 to 3 A.M.

POK (Paragraph OK?)

For each paragraph in your paper, ask:

- "Is it indented?"

- "Is it made up of sentences related to *one* main idea?"

- "Is it connected logically with paragraphs that come before or after?"

SOK (Sentence OK?)

For each sentence in your paper, ask:

- "Does it start with a capital letter?"

- "Does it end with the correct punctuation mark?"

- "Is other punctuation used correctly?" (Check commas, quotation marks, etc.)

- "Is it a complete sentence (not a fragment or run-on)?"

- "Does it express a complete thought?"

- "Do the subject and verb agree?"

- "Is its meaning clear?"

WOK (Word OK?)

For each word in your paper, ask:

- "Is it spelled correctly?"

- "Is it capitalized, if it needs to be?"

- "Is it used correctly?"

- "Is it overused?" (Have you used it too often in this paper?)

- "Is it slang?" (If it is, should it be?)

- "Is it the *very best* word, or is there another, better word I could use instead?"

Marc's edits

My Room And How It
Came To Be

It all started when my mother, sister,

and I went to an office supply store. I

don't remember why, but I'm glad we did.

recurred
While we were there the thought (recured)

recurred
to me (I say (recured) because my

parents and I had talked about it for

furniture
years) that I needed new (furnature)

(as in desk with a hutch & book case).

When I brought up the fact, my

sister (of course, as usual) decided that

she needed to get a desk too.

"I always tell people that I became a writer not because I went to school but because my mother took me to the library. I wanted to become a writer so I could see my name in the card catalog."

—SANDRA CISNEROS

NOK (Neatness OK?)

By now, you'll probably want to copy your paper over again (or print out another copy). Then ask yourself these questions, one at a time, reading through your paper with each question:

- "Does it follow the form required by my teacher?" (Typed and double-spaced? Written on only one side of the paper? With correct margins? With a cover sheet or title page? In a folder?)
- "If it's handwritten, have I used my best handwriting?" (Check size, shape, slant, and spacing of letters.)

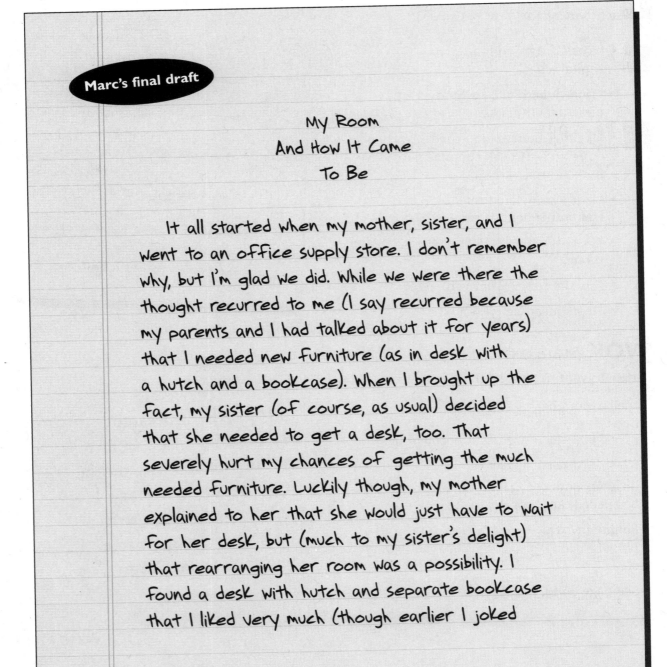

Marc's final draft

My Room
And How It Came
To Be

It all started when my mother, sister, and I went to an office supply store. I don't remember why, but I'm glad we did. While we were there the thought recurred to me (I say recurred because my parents and I had talked about it for years) that I needed new furniture (as in desk with a hutch and a bookcase). When I brought up the fact, my sister (of course, as usual) decided that she needed to get a desk, too. That severely hurt my chances of getting the much needed furniture. Luckily though, my mother explained to her that she would just have to wait for her desk, but (much to my sister's delight) that rearranging her room was a possibility. I found a desk with hutch and separate bookcase that I liked very much (though earlier I joked

Punctuation Pointers

 Commas separate items in a series, city and state, dates, and greetings and closings of friendly letters.

If I win the lottery, I will buy the most expensive clothes I can find: jeans, running shoes, and jackets.

I was born in Akron, Ohio. My birthday was January 15, 1990.

Dear Chip,
Blah blah blah

Your friend,
Dale

 Exclamation points show excitement!!!!!

 Question marks show the ends of questions.

Wow! Can you really bench-press 200 pounds?

Periods go at the ends of sentences that don't need an **!** or a **?**, and after abbreviations.

Dr. Smith and her friend, Mrs. Black, rushed to the rally.

Quotation marks show the beginning and the end of what someone says. Periods and commas *always* go *inside* quotation marks. Semicolons and colons usually go *outside* quotation marks.

"I won't," he said calmly, in no uncertain terms. "I simply won't." His mother's stony response was, "You will"; his father remained silent.

 Semicolons separate main ideas, and items in series that already have commas.

Colons go before a list or an example. They're also used in greetings of business letters.

On his incredible sandwich, Dagwood piled cheeses: Swiss, American, and cheddar; vegetables: lettuce, hot peppers, and cucumbers; and meats: ham and turkey.

Dear Sir or Madam:

Parentheses surround extra comments added (like this one) into sentences.

If You're Not Sure About Your S-p-e-l-l-i-n-g

- Use a spellchecker program if you're writing on a computer that has one.

- Use a dictionary. A regular dictionary may be hard to use, since you need to know how to spell a word before you can look it up. Instead, try one of these special dictionaries. Check your bookstore or order a copy online, or ask your bookstore to order a copy for you.

How to Spell It: A Dictionary of Commonly Misspelled Words by Harriet Wittels and Joan Greisman (New York: Price Stern Sloan Publishing, 1982). A word list (no definitions) that includes both correct and incorrect spellings. Look up a word the way you *think* it should be spelled, and you'll find the *correct* way it's spelled.

Random House Webster's Pocket Bad Speller's Dictionary by Joseph Krevisky and Jordan Linfield (New York: Random House, 1998). Arranges words alphabetically according to their common misspellings.

- See page 80 for tips on becoming a better speller.

How to Write Paragraphs

- Make sure that all the sentences are on the same topic. Make sure they're arranged in an order that makes sense.

- Avoid one-sentence paragraphs. Each paragraph should be long enough to develop its topic.

- Does the paragraph go on and on? Maybe you should break it up into two (or more) paragraphs. Maybe you're trying to say too much. Maybe you're wandering off your topic.

- If you're writing a paragraph that explains something, ask yourself, "What would I learn if I were reading this for the first time?"

- If you're writing a descriptive paragraph, ask yourself, "What would I 'see' if I were reading this for the first time?"

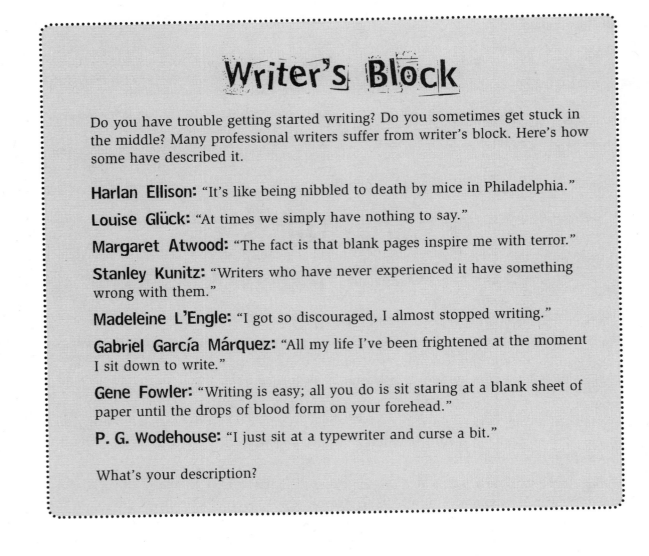

Writer's Block

Do you have trouble getting started writing? Do you sometimes get stuck in the middle? Many professional writers suffer from writer's block. Here's how some have described it.

Harlan Ellison: "It's like being nibbled to death by mice in Philadelphia."

Louise Glück: "At times we simply have nothing to say."

Margaret Atwood: "The fact is that blank pages inspire me with terror."

Stanley Kunitz: "Writers who have never experienced it have something wrong with them."

Madeleine L'Engle: "I got so discouraged, I almost stopped writing."

Gabriel García Márquez: "All my life I've been frightened at the moment I sit down to write."

Gene Fowler: "Writing is easy; all you do is sit staring at a blank sheet of paper until the drops of blood form on your forehead."

P. G. Wodehouse: "I just sit at a typewriter and curse a bit."

What's your description?

Writer's Block BUSTERS

- Copy a few paragraphs or pages from your favorite book.

- Imitate your favorite writer's style.

- Try writing in a style that's new to you. How about an adventure? A science fiction story? A sword-and-sorcerers fantasy? A romance? A Western? A mystery? Explore new ground. You may discover new writing talents.

- Draw a picture of your writer's block. Use your imagination. It doesn't matter *what* you draw, just *that* you draw. The act of drawing gets your "whole brain" working and stimulates creative thinking.

How to Write Stories

A story should entertain, inform, interest, or amuse your audience. Your readers should care about what happens to your characters.

- **The Setting.** Where does your story happen? When? Give the geographical location and the specific place of each scene (outdoors, in someone's house, in a museum). Think about how long your story takes (a single day, weeks, a hundred years). Include lots of colorful details. For example, the story of Robin Hood takes place in Sherwood Forest a long time ago.

- **The Characters.** Tell your readers what your characters look like. Describe their personalities. Most of all, make them interesting! Is Friar Tuck holy, roly-poly, and humorous? Would you want to go hunting with Maid Marian? What color hair does Robin have, and does he wear green tights or leather pants?

- **The Problem and Solution.** Present a problem and lead up to the solution. The Sheriff of Nottingham is overtaxing the people of England, a big problem for them. Robin Hood solves it by taking from the rich, giving to the poor—and besting the Sheriff.

- **The Events.** Describe five or six events. Present them in an order that makes sense. (The order you arrange events is called the *plot* of your story.) You can't have Robin give to the poor *before* he takes from the rich. A story map can help you plan your story. On pages 118–119, you'll find a Story Map you can copy and use.

How to Write Essays

An essay is a short work of nonfiction. It can be a single paragraph or several pages long. In an essay, you express an idea, give and support an opinion, or develop an idea.

A letter to the editor is an essay. So are some newspaper and magazine articles. So are most papers written in high school and college. When you state your opinion during a conversation, and back it up with facts and information, you're giving an oral essay.

Follow this form for writing essays.

1. First, say what you're going to say (what your essay will be about).
2. Next, say it (the body of your essay).

   - Stick to the topic. Even a very long, very neat paper won't make the grade if it doesn't stay on track.
   - Make your organization obvious. Use clue words like "first," "next," "on the other hand," "furthermore," "also," "in conclusion," and so on.
   - Say what you mean, and mean what you say. Your teacher can't read your mind.

3. Finally, say what you said (conclusion).

Also, see pages 92–93 for tips on writing essay tests. The forms on pages 126–127 can help you plan informational writing.

How to Write Poems

Poetry is the oldest form of literature. Before people could write—before alphabets were invented—they made up poems and told them to one another. Many cultures preserved their history in long poems, passed down from one storyteller to the next.

You may think that poetry comes with lots of rules. Some forms do. For example, if you want to write like Shakespeare, you'll need to learn iambic pentameter—a special kind of rhythm. If you want to write limericks, you'll need to know that a limerick is a five-line poem with a definite rhythm and rhyme.

There was a young student from Nome
Whose teacher assigned a long poem.
Though he stayed up all night,
This is all he could write.
Here ends the young Nome student's poem.

In general, a poem expresses a feeling: love, humor, anger, you name it. Most poems have an inner "beat" or rhythm, like a song or a rap.

Poems *don't* have to be mushy. Shel Silverstein wrote funny poems; Jack Prelutsky writes gory poems. Different poets have different "voices," themes, and styles.

Poems *don't* have to rhyme. As a matter of fact, forcing a rhyme can lead to truly awful poetry.

I ate a cake
that mom had to bake.
What a mistake!

Mostly, a poem you write must say something *you* want to say. It should speak with *your* voice. Since poems usually have fewer words than essays or stories, you must choose your words carefully. Try many different words until you find the right ones for your poem.

Like other forms of writing, a poem should have a definite topic, purpose, and audience. Your teacher may assign a specific form—for example, a haiku. Make sure that you understand exactly what kind of poem your teacher expects you to write. Ask to see samples.

If you're free to choose any form you like, try one of the following. They may not win any prizes, but they'll help get you started.

Adjective Poem

1. List four adjectives about yourself. For example: cool, shy, fun-loving, skinny.

2. List four adjectives about the person you'd most like to be your friend. For example: outgoing, friendly, athletic, popular.

3. Now stack your adjectives like blocks:

Cool
Shy
Fun-loving
Skinny
Outgoing
Friendly
Athletic
Popular

Prepositional Poem

1. Make a list of prepositions: **2.** Turn each one into a phrase:

In	Over	In the dark woods	Over the hill
Under	Beneath	Under a maple tree	Beneath the bright blue sky
On	Near	On the grass	Near home

Don't be shy. Let yourself go! You may think that poems are impossible to write. In fact, poetry gives you more freedom to experiment and play with the words than almost any other kind of writing.

"Found" Poem

1. Look through magazines and newspapers for words and phrases that catch your eye.

2. Cut them out and arrange them on a piece of paper. Move them around until you like what you see.

3. Paste them down for posterity.

Feeling the heat

Ouch!

Neck-deep

Cool as ice

Feed the flames

Such sweet sorrow

How to Write a Book Report

First, *read the book.* Accept no substitutes. Don't settle for the movie or a friend's book report. The book is the real thing.

Next, follow the format your teacher gives you. If your teacher doesn't provide specific instructions, copy and use one of the forms for writing book reports on fiction, nonfiction, and biographies on pages 120–125.

Or, try one of these fun alternatives. (Clear it with your teacher ahead of time.)

- Make a book jacket. Create art for the cover. Write the text for the back and the flaps.
- Write a sequel or prequel to the book. What do you think happens after the last page of the book? What do you think happened before the first page?
- Create a collage about the book.
- Make a poster advertising the book.
- Write a slogan promoting the book.
- Design a T-shirt about the book.
- Come up with your own idea.

Should You Write on a Computer?

If you have one (or access to one), use it! Depending on your software, your computer can:

- make it easier to organize, add, take out, and move information
- check and correct your spelling
- center your titles
- point out errors in grammar and punctuation
- hyphenate words correctly
- set margins all around your paper
- do illustrations, such as pie and bar graphs

This book was written on a computer, edited on a computer, and designed on a computer. So you can see some of what computers can do.

But no computer or software can think or correct spelling mistakes that are real words. You'll still have to make the decisions about what to write and how to write it. (It may *look* great when it rolls out of the printer, but how it reads is up to you.) And your computer won't change "in" to "on," "no" to "know," "dessert" to "desert," etc. Even so, computers are terrific time-savers.

How to Write a Research Paper

You walk into class and there it is in giant letters on the chalkboard:

WRITE A 10-PAGE PAPER ON GERBILS. DUE IN THREE WEEKS.

It's a big job, but *you've* got to do it. And you'll need to call on most of your *School Power* skills: getting organized, taking notes, reading, and writing.

- Make sure that you understand the assignment. If you don't, ask.

- Find out all the requirements for the paper. Will it need a title page? A table of contents? A bibliography? Pictures, illustrations, maps, or other graphics? Should it be typed? Double spaced?

- Pick a topic. Even if the teacher assigns the main topic, you should be able to choose your own angle. For example, if the main topic is "Recycling," you may want to focus on aluminum cans. The trick is to pick a topic that's broad and narrow at the same time. If it's too narrow—for example, "The Eating Habits of Parakeets in Frostproof, Florida"—you may not find any information at all.

> "Research is . . . poking and prying with purpose."
> —Zora Neale Hurston

- Turn your topic into a thesis sentence that summarizes what you plan to write about. Examples: "Football is the most popular sport in the United States." "Women aren't paid as much as men for the same kind of work." Have your teacher approve this sentence.

- Research your topic in the library. Skim and scan many sources of information. Don't limit yourself to encyclopedias. If you can't find what you need, ask the librarian for help. *Carefully* write down your sources. You'll need them later for your bibliography.

- Check the Internet for additional articles or information.

- Contact community resources related to your topic. This is a great way to add originality to your paper. You might collect posters of different countries from a travel agency. Or ask ethnic restaurants for menus. Or learn about a profession by contacting its professional association. Or interview experts in your own community. For interview tips, see pages 40–41.

- Write letters to request information from national sources. Find sources and addresses in your library's reference section.

- Take notes on the materials you find or receive. Write them on index cards so you can put them in order later.

- Plan your paper using suggestions on page 64.

- Write a rough draft, following your plan. Revise your outline if you need to.

- Revise and edit your rough draft with MOK, POK, SOK, and WOK from A-OK (see pages 68–70).

- Write your final draft with NOK from A-OK.

See pages 126–127 for a Research Paper Checklist you can copy and use.

The Goldilocks Rule

If you have a tough time coming up with a topic, try this exercise:

1. Brainstorm as many ideas as you can in five minutes. Use a timer.
2. Write down all of your ideas. Don't stop to read or judge them.
3. When the timer goes off, stop.
4. Organize your ideas with the Goldilocks Rule:
   - (1) = Too Broad
   - (2) = Too Narrow
   - (3) = Just Right
5. Pick a topic from the Just Right category.

Your Bibliography

Your teacher might give you instructions on how to write your bibliography. Your English textbook should also provide examples. You should know that there are several different styles for citing references: MLA, APA, and Chicago, to name a few. There are formats for all types of print sources: books, magazine articles, encyclopedia entries, book chapters, and newspaper articles. Use the format that your teacher recommends. If he or she does not recommend a format, pick one and use it consistently.

Now there are even ways to cite information you find on the Internet (such as emails, Web sites, book reviews, etc.). An excellent starting place for finding ways to document information gathered from the Internet is a Web site called Online! Check it out at: (*www.bedfordstmartins.com/online/citex.html*).

The important thing is to document *all* the resources you used to write your paper. Do *not* copy someone else's work. Use quotation marks around material you copy and give credit to the originator of the information. Make certain you create a bibliography that lists all the references you used.

"The best of my education has come from the public library. . . . My tuition fee is a bus fare and once in awhile, five cents a day for an overdue book. You don't need to know very much to start with, if you know the way to the public library."

—LESLEY CONGER

How to Be a Better Speller

Some people are terrible spellers. But most of us can learn to be better spellers, if we try. Being a better speller will make writing easier for you. It'll save you time. And when spelling counts as part of your grade, it'll earn you points.

- Pay attention to how words are spelled. Do this when you read *and* when you write.

- Keep a personal list of new and difficult words. See pages 36–37 for suggestions.

- Play word games. Try Scrabble, Boggle, UpWords, Scattergories, and Hangman.

- If your family has a handheld electronic dictionary, use it to play word games.

- Teachers and other reading specialists have made lists of Spelling Demons—words that seem to give students the most trouble. You'll find two "demon lists" on pages 128 and 129. Make copies for your notebook and the bulletin board in your home study center. Ask your friends and family to practice the words with you. (They make great Hangman puzzles.)

- Set up a schedule for studying spelling words.

Spelling Study

On the day spelling words are assigned

✔ Test yourself on the words for that week. Find out which ones you'll need to study.

For the rest of the week

✔ Schedule regular study sessions for every day or every other day. Keep them short—no more than 15–20 minutes. Several short sessions are more effective than a night-before-the-test cram-a-thon.

✔ Squeeze brief practices into spare moments—in the car, while you're waiting to be picked up from soccer practice, on the bus, during breakfast.

On the night before the test

✔ Review all the words—the hard ones and the easy ones.

✔ Get help studying. Have a friend or family member dictate your spelling words to you. Write them down, leaving a blank space underneath each. Afterward, check your work. For any misspelled word, write the correct spelling under the incorrect spelling.

✔ Or, record your own test tape. Dictate your words, leaving a pause after each, so you can write it down.

✔ Make up *mnemonics*—memory tricks—to help you remember spelling words. You already know "i before e except after c." Try remembering "piece" as a *piece* of *pie*. See page 87 for more mnemonic examples.

✔ Write *all* of your spelling words once. Then write them all again . . . and again . . . until you've mastered them. Don't count on remembering words you only spell out loud. You need to write them.

✔ Use computer programs like Crossword Magic to create crossword puzzles from your spelling words.

STUDY
SMARTER

HOW TO STUDY

Adults talk about two facts of life they can't escape: death and taxes. Two facts of school life come close: tests and homework.

You can run, but you can't hide. And unless have a photographic memory, there's just one way to make the grade: buckle down and study.

✔ Post a DO NOT DISTURB sign.

✔ Look over everything you need to do, and write a study plan.

✔ If you have a lot to study, plan several short sessions with breaks. You'll be more productive.

✔ Is there anything you'll need help with? Tell your study partner or parent. Schedule time together. *Don't* wait until the last minute.

✔ Do the tough assignments first, when you're fresh.

✔ Vary your study activities. Read for a while, then write, then do math problems, then memorize, then read again.

✔ Save the last few minutes for a final review of test material or material you need to memorize.

Do you have trouble remembering what you study? See page 87 for memory boosters.

Ways to Improve Your Concentration

Some people can concentrate for long periods of time. But even if your attention span is short, you *can* keep your mind on something you're *really* interested in. And you can improve your ability to concentrate if you're willing to work on it.

1 Follow the suggestions on pages 4–6 for setting up a home study center. Try to make your study center a special place *only* for studying—no noise, toys, or distractions.

2 Start with only short study sessions. Increase your study time by five to ten minutes each day until you reach your goal.

3 Set small goals and reward yourself when you reach them.

4 Try your hardest to get interested in what you're studying. If a subject is boring to you, find a friend who likes it and ask why. Read a magazine article, watch a video about it, or surf the Internet for material on that subject. Come up with questions to ask your teacher in class.

5 Some of us are "larks"—morning people. Some of us are "owls"— night people. Owls hate to study in the morning, and larks fall asleep at night. What's your peak time? Study then.

6 Keep active. Take notes, underline, write down questions, highlight, draw diagrams, read aloud, and ask yourself questions.

7 If you start to fade or daydream, stop. Stand up, stretch, jump up and down, munch an apple—or take a short nap, if you really need it.

Study Plan Practice

You have six assignments to complete tonight. What order will you do them in? Why?

_____ Work ten long-division problems and three word problems.

_____ Study a chapter for a science test.

_____ Write a short story for English class.

_____ Read a chapter for social studies.

_____ Ask your parents to sign the permission form for your class field trip.

_____ Define 15 words for computer class.

How to ▶ Start a Study Group

Many students like to study with their friends. It's less lonely and more fun. Plus, a study group can help everyone do better on tests—as long as all members do their share of the work.

- Limit your group to three or four students. Pick students who stay awake in class, ask questions, and take notes.

- Give the group a tryout with a one-time-only study session. If it seems to work, plan another session or set a regular meeting time.

- Shorter, more frequent meetings are better than once-a-month cram-a-thons.

Before the Study Session

1. Draw up an agenda (meeting plan). Decide what material to cover.

2. Plug each topic into a time frame. For example, 15 minutes for science, 20 minutes for social studies and history.

3. Assign each group member a part of the material to study. It's that person's responsibility to "teach" it to the rest of the group. Your study session will be made up of several "mini-lessons."

4. Get ready to teach your own mini-lesson. Read all assigned material or class notes. Identify any problem areas. Make up test questions to ask the group.

During the Study Session

1. Start by going over the agenda. Set or review group rules.

2. Ask for a volunteer to be an "agenda monitor." That person will keep track of time and make sure the group doesn't wander off the topic.

3. Go through the mini-lessons. Group members should feel free to ask questions and add material that isn't covered. Each "teacher" should stop every few minutes or so, checking to see that group members understand the material being presented.

4. End each mini-lesson with practice test questions. Brainstorm more questions.

5. End the session by reviewing major ideas and problem areas.

Give Yourself a Study Checkup

Are your grades not as good as you think they should be? Do you sometimes have trouble taking tests? Maybe you need a study checkup.

Page 130 has a form you can copy and use to find out how healthy your study habits are. Fill one out during your next study session. It'll help you see how you're spending your time. Maybe you're skipping something you should be doing. You're the doctor. You decide.

Nick's Tip for Study Groups

Whenever Nick had a group assignment, he and his group usually ended up working in the library. Nick liked this so well that he decided to study in the library with friends, even when their assignments were individual ones. They still hold their study group meetings at the library, too.

How to → Remember What You Study

You spend hours studying for a test, alone or in a group. Then the big day arrives—suddenly your mind is a black hole. It can happen to anyone. You can prevent it by adding these memory boosters to your study sessions:

Recite. Read aloud. Recite what you're learning to yourself, a study partner, or a parent. Hearing and speaking can help information stick in your mind.

Use mnemonics. Make up words, names, or sentences to help you remember facts and ideas. For example:

> To remember a sequence, use a sentence or key words. For the colors of the spectrum, memorize **ROY G. BIV**—Red, Orange, Yellow, Green, Blue, Indigo, and Violet.

> To remember a date, try a rhyme. ("In 1492, Columbus sailed the ocean blue . . .")

> To remember the meaning of a word, associate it with something you know. For "obnoxious," you might think of the school bully.

Overlearn. Keep studying something even after you know it. Overlearning is especially useful if you get very nervous during tests.

Visualize. Picture what the information looks like on the page you're studying. Make mental pictures of facts and ideas. Draw real pictures, if that helps you to learn.

Apply what you learn. If you use it, you won't lose it. For example, if you read a computer manual and then practice the program, you'll remember much better than if you just stick with the reading.

Cathy's Tip for Remembering

Cathy sometimes had trouble remembering what she read. She started reading aloud to herself. She finds that this helps her to remember more. She may not always want to read aloud to herself, but for now, this technique works for her.

Turn Learning into a Game

Learning is serious business, but it doesn't have to be serious *all of the time.* There are many ways to learn besides studying and sitting in class.

Stretch your brain, strengthen your funny bone, build your skills, and add to your knowledge base with these entertaining games. Play with friends and family or challenge yourself. Your study group may decide that a game is a great way to end a study session. Here's a list of commercially available games you may want to try:

ASAP Card Game

Half the cards present categories: movies, U.S. cities, nonsense words, something green, and so on. The rest of the cards contain letters of the alphabet. Lay them out and players have to think quickly to come up with words or names that fit both the subject and the designated first letter.

Boggle

A small container holds 16 cubes, each cube is marked with a different letter on each of its six sides. Shake the container and let the cubes land within the little pockets. The object is to find as many words (of three or more letters) as you can—in three minutes.

Where in the World Is Carmen Sandiego?

Each story begins with a dispatched message from the Chief. She tells you what you need to know: what was stolen, who to look for, and where you're being sent to catch the thief. The purpose is to build a profile of the criminal and to learn the history of your destination spots. Builds geography skills. A computer software game, available in several versions for many kinds of computers.

Risk

This is a game of world conquest and features a game board that's a map of six continents divided into 42 territories. It's a game of strategy and you battle to win by launching attacks and defending your territory against your opponent. Builds geography and strategic thinking skills.

Taboo

This is a timed game in which one player tries to get teammates to guess a word or phrase—*but* there are some words and phrases the player can't say. For example: you want your teammates to guess the word "sink," *but* you can't use the words "swim," "kitchen," "water," "disposal," or "faucet" as clues. Or you want your teammates to guess the phrase "World Series." *But* you can't say "baseball," "game," "National League," "American League," or "champions" as clues. This game helps to build vocabulary.

Jeopardy

Just like the TV trivia game show, there are three rounds of play. Because the subject matter is widely varied, it offers a medley that works well even with a mixed age group. Builds general knowledge. Available as a board game or video game.

Trivial Pursuit & Jr. Trivial Pursuit

What food gives Popeye strength? What country calls its native inhabitants "aborigines"? What street sport sees cuts and scrapes from falls called "munchies"? These trivia games are available in several versions and themes. Builds general knowledge.

Beyond Balderdash

There are five categories of questions (words, people, initials, movies, and dates). A question is selected from one of the categories and each player writes down an answer, either trying to answer the question correctly or hoping to bluff the other players with an inventive, believable-sounding answer.

Outburst Junior

A timed trivia game—name all the Jell-O flavors you can think of in 60 seconds. How many books by Judy Blume can you remember? Each team is given one minute to shout out answers that might—or might not—be listed on the topic card. For every correct answer, the team scores one point. Builds general knowledge. You can also try the adult version.

How to ▶ Predict Test Questions

If you can predict the test questions your teacher will ask, and if you practice your answers, you *will* do better on tests. The CHANCE strategy can help you predict possible test questions. It's the next best thing to a crystal ball.

C = Critical ideas

Focus on the *critical ideas*—the ones that are most important to understanding the chapter or topic as a whole. Most teachers won't test you on the picky details.

H = Higher-order questions

Some questions require answers that are very clear. You can find the answers right in your class notes or textbooks. These are called *lower-order questions*. For example, "Which president's wife held seances?" "When did the *Lusitania* sink?"

But other questions require more thinking. You have to pull information from more than one sentence or paragraph, make judgments, or draw conclusions. These are called *higher-order questions*. For example, "What would happen if a president's wife or husband held seances today?" "How might history have been different if the *Lusitania* had not been sunk?"

When preparing for a test, try to predict both kinds of questions.

A = Accuracy

Do you understand the material you're studying? If you can tell in your own words what a textbook chapter said, or explain what your teacher meant during a class lecture, then you're interpreting these materials with *accuracy*. The questions you predict will be more accurate, too.

N = Number

Don't predict just one or two questions. Predict a large *number*—as many as you can. Cover all of the material you're studying. The more answers you can practice, the better you'll do.

C = Clarity

Confusing questions lead to confusing answers. Are your questions clear? Do they have *clarity*? You can improve the clarity of your questions by choosing your words carefully. For example, "What are the five major causes of the Civil War?" has more clarity (and leads to better answers) than, "What are the reasons the Civil War started?"

E = Examine

Use your predicted questions to *examine* yourself. Make up and take a sample test. Check your answers against your textbook notes.

How to Psych Yourself Up for a Test

It's the night before the "Big Test." You've been studying for days. What can you do to get in the mood for tomorrow? Start by going to bed. Get a good night's sleep. In the morning, eat a healthy breakfast. Save the Sweet 'n' Sticky Belly Bombs for another day, so you won't sugar-crash in mid-test. Dress in comfy clothes. Listen to your favorite music while you're getting ready for school.

In other words, take care of yourself. No secrets here! Before leaving home, make sure you have everything you need for the test. You may want to make a mini-checklist:

✔ pencils

✔ pens

✔ paper

✔ books (if you can use them during the test)

✔ calculator

✔ (anything else?)

Try to arrive a few minutes early. On the way, tell yourself "I'm ready. I'll do my best—and that'll be good enough for me."

Diana Lia's Tip for Checking Your Work

Diana Lia checks her answers with friends before turning in her assignments. Sometimes the teacher doesn't get around to correcting all the homework. This way, Diana and her friends know if they're at least on the right track. They aren't surprised when test time comes.

When to Cram for a Test

The best time to cram for a test is . . .

a. the night before

b. the morning of

c. neither

The answer is "c." It's tempting to leave your studying to the last minute, and you might remember some of what you stuff into your brain, but you won't remember it for long. You may not even remember it during the test.

Instead of cramming, give yourself plenty of time to review. Start on the day the test is announced.

- Go over everything at least once—textbooks, class notes, old tests, and quizzes.

- Memorize lists, formulas, and definitions. Use mnemonics (see page 87).

- Pay special attention to problem areas. If possible, get help from a friend or family member.

- Learn the correct spellings of key terms and technical words.

- Make up a sample test. Answer the questions. Check your answers.

Kate's Tip for Getting Ready for Tests

Kate uses flash cards for every subject—even math. Every subject requires that she learns new vocabulary. She puts the word on the front of the card and the definition on the back. It really works for her. Sometimes if it's going to be a hard test, her mom runs through the flash cards with her. The best thing about flash cards is that they're portable. She can study them on the bus, in bed, anywhere!

Five Ways to Conquer Test Anxiety

1 Memorize important facts, figures, formulas, and dates ahead of time. Then, just before starting the test, do a "splashdown" on the back of your paper. Quickly write down anything you'll need for the test. Later, if anxiety creeps in, you'll still have important information at your fingertips.

2 Practice the test-taking strategies in this section. The more prepared you are, the less anxious you'll feel.

3 If you start getting anxious, take a brief relaxation break. Close your eyes. Breathe deeply. Think about tensing, then relaxing, every part of your body from your toes to the top of your head.

4 If other students finish before you do, ignore them. It's a myth that top students finish first, average students finish in the middle, and poor students finish last.

5 If you finish early, use the time to check your answers.

How to ➤ Take Essay Tests

Essay tests can be the pits. First you have to understand the question. Then you have to figure out the answer. Then you have to remember information that fits the answer. Then you have to organize it in a way that makes sense. Then you have to write it down. All within a time limit! You can't escape essay tests. But you can make them easier to take.

Before the Test

Practice PORPE, a five-step way to prepare for essay tests on any subject.

P = Predict
Predict test questions using the CHANCE strategy on page 89. Ask your friends or study group to predict questions. The more questions you can come up with, the better.

O = Organize
Organize the information needed to answer the questions. Use diagrams, outlines, charts—whatever works. See pages 64–66 for ideas.

R = Rehearse
Review the memory boosters on page 87. Recite the information in your diagrams, outlines, or charts. Repeat over the next several days so the information sticks in your long-term memory.

P = Practice
Practice writing the answers to your predicted questions. Time yourself to model test conditions. Quickly jot down important ideas, and sketch your diagrams, outlines, or charts from memory. Add examples and facts to back up your ideas.

Because your teacher may give you different types of essay questions, practice writing different types of answers. Examples: "Discuss . . . ," "Explain . . . ," "Describe . . . ," and "Compare and contrast . . ."

Check the overall organization of your answers. For each, is there an introduction? A conclusion? Does it make sense? Have you included all major points? Have you said what you really wanted to say?

E = Evaluate
Go over your answers with a teacher's eye. How could they be better? What have you forgotten? What have you done especially well? Evaluating answers is a good activity for your study group to do together.

- Read all of the questions. Do a quick "splashdown" on the back of your paper or a piece of scrap paper. Jot down any names, facts, dates, and anything else you think you'll need for your essays. Or brainstorm words related to your topic, and group them in a cluster.

  physical fitness, exercise, not flabby, eat right, good endurance, sleep enough

- Follow directions *exactly*. You'll stay out of trouble and you may save time. For example, if you're instructed to "define" or "summarize" a topic, that usually means you can write a brief answer. "Discuss," "explain," or "describe" calls for a longer answer. "Compare and contrast" means what it says: tell how two things are the same *and* how they are different. For tips on following written directions, see page 57.

- Write your essay. If you think you have time, write it first on scrap paper, proofread it, make any changes, then copy it onto your test paper. For tips on writing essays, see page 74.

- Read your essay to make sure it makes sense.

The STAR Strategy for Test Success

STAR is a simple four-letter formula that's especially useful for timed tests.

- **Survey** the test to get an idea of how much time you can spend on each question, and which questions you can answer quickly. Pay attention to the number of points per question.

- **Take** time to read the directions *carefully*. Studies have shown that poor test-takers tend to misread directions and questions.

- **Answer** the questions. Start with an easy one to boost your confidence.

- **Reread** the questions and your answers. Make any needed changes.

Tips for Taking Objective Tests

There are many different kinds of objective tests: true-false, multiple-choice, fill-in-the-blank, matching, and so on. True-false and fill-in-the-blank are the trickiest.

True-False

- If *any* part of a statement is false, then *all* of the statement is false.

- Watch for absolute words like "all," "none," "only," "always," and "never." They can be clues that an answer is false. Few things are "always" or "never" so.

- Watch for weasel words like "usually," "generally," "often," "seldom," "some," and "may." They can be clues that an answer is true.

Multiple Choice

- Read each possible answer *with* the stem. This will help you focus on the right answer to the question that you're given.

    Example: Many teenagers like:
    a. to listen to loud music
    b. to wear clothes that are "in"
    c. to be on their own
    d. to go to parties
    e. all of the above

    You would read this question in five ways:
    a. (Many teenagers like) to listen to loud music.
    b. (Many teenagers like) to wear clothes that are "in."
    c. (Many teenagers like) to be on their own.
    d. (Many teenagers like) to go to parties.
    e. (Many teenagers like) all of the above.

- Read *all* choices before picking an answer. In the example above, "a" seems okay, but it's not the *best* answer; "e" is.

- Use the process of elimination. If you know that "b," "d," and "e," are wrong, then the answer must be "a" or "c."

- When in doubt, guess. Your guess may be right; leaving a blank won't be. *Exception:* Some standardized tests have a penalty for guessing. Check with your teacher.

- If one choice is much longer than the rest, and it seems likely to be right, go with it. Longer answers tend to be right more often than shorter answers.

- If two of the choices are exact opposites, pick one of them.

   Example: What happens when you add salt to water before boiling it?
   a. It turns the hydrogen in the water to helium.
   b. It makes the water boil faster.
   c. It makes the water boil slower.
   d. It turns to salt crystals.
   e. Nothing happens.

   Notice that "b" and "c" are opposites. Pick "b."

- When you don't have a clue what the right answer is, pick "c" first. If you think "c" may be wrong, pick "b" or "d." Teachers like to sandwich the right answer between other choices, so avoid "a" or "e."

What If You're Not Sure of Your Answer?

You read the question and quickly write an answer that you *think* is right. But you're not *positive* it's right. What should you do? Many people would say, "Leave it. Your first impression is best." But a University of Michigan professor says, "Change it."

Dr. Frank Whitehouse did a study on tests turned in by more than 1,000 of his students over the past ten years. He looked for eraser marks and other signs that students had changed their answers. He found that students changed from wrong to right answers 2.5 times as often as they changed from right to wrong.

After you answer a question, you may find that later questions contain clues to the first question. Or you may remember an important fact later in the test. Or you may just think twice about your first answer, and feel strongly that you should change it. Don't let superstition about "first impressions" hold you back.

What to Do When the Test Comes Back

When the teacher hands your test back, don't just stick it in your notebook or desk. You can learn a lot from a PTA—Post-Test Analysis.

- Look at each error. Try to figure out why you made it. Was it a careless mistake? Did you forget to study something, or forget something you studied?

- Find out the right answer for each question you missed. Write it on your test paper. Turn it into a study tool for next time.

- Keep a file of old tests. They can help you predict the kinds of questions your teacher likes to ask.

How to ➤ Survive Standardized Tests

Standardized tests are a pain. Why should you have to take them? Because many adults feel the need to evaluate you and your school. Standardized tests compare your performance to that of other students in your district, state, or country.

You can try to prepare for standardized tests. You can work on improving your vocabulary all year long. (See pages 36–37 for tips on learning new words.) You can take practice tests at school. Or you can decide not to worry about standardized tests until you have to take them. Then just do your best, and forget about them afterward.

- Use the techniques on page 91 for conquering test anxiety. Reread the section, How to Psych Yourself Up for a Test, on page 90. Review the tips for taking multiple-choice tests on pages 94–95.

- Most standardized tests use a test booklet and a special answer sheet. You fill in the bubbles on the answer sheet. There are many questions, so you should make sure that the question number matches the answer number you're filling in. It's easy to lose track.

- If you are right-handed, keep your answer sheet on the right side of your test booklet. This way, you won't waste time crossing your hand over your test booklet after each answer.

- If you are left-handed, keep your answer sheet on the left side of your test booklet for the same reason.

- If you change your mind about an answer, erase your mark carefully, and don't leave any stray marks on the paper. Standardized tests are scored by machines that don't know the difference between filled in answers and accidental pencil marks.

- Reading comprehension tests almost always have "main idea" questions. These may be disguised as "most important" or "topic" questions. As you read, keep an eye out for key main ideas, especially at the beginning and/or end of each paragraph.

Standardized tests are only *one* measure of how you're doing in school. Your day-to-day work is a much better measure. Most teachers know that. So don't stay awake nights thinking about standardized tests. Focus on keeping up with your homework, read a lot, and do your best on classroom tests. You'll do just fine.

Kate, Kyle, Jeff, and Charlie's Tip for Getting Ready for Standardized Tests

All four kids agree—the best way to prepare for standardized tests is to listen in class and follow your teachers' directions about how to prepare. As Kate puts it, "The tests are really on things you learned all year long. If you pay attention and do the practice sheets the teachers give you, you should be okay." Charlie says, "Most of my teachers give us a lot of practice on important things that'll be on the test. We have a big state writing test. They give you some topics—or prompts—and you have to write an essay or story based on that topic. I do all the practice exercises and my teacher lets me know what I need to work on."

Tools for School Success

Time Management Chart

	Monday	Tuesday	Wednesday	Thursday	Friday	Saturday	Sunday
8:00							
9:00							
10:00							
11:00							
12:00							
1:00							
2:00							
3:00							
4:00							
5:00							
6:00							
7:00							
8:00							
9:00							
10:00							
11:00							

Assignment Sheet

WEEK OF:					
Date of Assignment	Subject	Book or Project	Page	Date Due	Grade

Daily Planning Worksheet

THINGS TO DO ON:		
Priorities	Daily homework assignments	Tasks to complete for long-range assignments
Phone calls, emails, and letters	Flyers and papers for parents to read/sign	Clubs & Activities
Personal activities	Home chores/tasks	Other

Project Plan

1. Decide on a project theme.   Date done: _____

2. Have the theme approved by your teacher.   Date done: _____

Theme: _____

3. Make a list of things you need to do to complete your project. Rank them in the order they should be completed.

_____   _____

_____   _____

_____   _____

_____   _____

4. Decide if you'll need help from your parents or other adults. Ask if and when they can help you. Be clear about what you want them to do.

Will need help with: **Who will help me:**

_____   _____

_____   _____

_____   _____

_____   _____

_____   _____

5. Set deadlines for finishing each part of your project. Write the deadline dates on your calendar.

Task	Date due	Date done	Person responsible
_____	_____	_____	_____
_____	_____	_____	_____
_____	_____	_____	_____
_____	_____	_____	_____
_____	_____	_____	_____

More >>

Project Plan (continued)

6. Make a list of materials you'll need. Estimate how much they'll cost.

Item   Cost

_____   _____

_____   _____

_____   _____

7. Send away for resource materials.

Resource material   Date requested   Date received

_____   _____   _____

_____   _____   _____

_____   _____   _____

8. Contact community resources.

Community resource   Date contacted   Result(s)

_____   _____   _____

_____   _____   _____

_____   _____   _____

9. Visit the library.

Purpose of visit   Date of visit

_____   _____

_____   _____

_____   _____

10. Check the Internet for related Web sites.

Web addresses   Date site visited

_____   _____

_____   _____

_____   _____

11. Complete your project on schedule.

Date turned in: _____   **Grade:** _____

My Goals for the → School Year

Today's date: _____

My goals for the school year:

1. _____

2. _____

3. _____

Reasons why I *can* achieve my goals:

1. _____

2. _____

3. _____

Reasons why I *might not* achieve my goals:

1. _____

2. _____

3. _____

Ways I *can* overcome or solve these problems:

1. _____

2. _____

3. _____

My Goals for the School Year

UPDATE

Today's date: _____

New or changed goals:

1. _____

2. _____

3. _____

Problems I overcame or solved:

1. _____

2. _____

3. _____

Other successes so far:

1. _____

2. _____

3. _____

FLIP Chart

Title of assignment: _____

Number of pages: _____

General directions: Rate each of the FLIP categories on a scale from 1–5 (5 = high, 1 = low). Circle your choice on the scale.

 = Friendliness: "How friendly is my reading assignment?"

Examine your assignment to see if it includes these friendly features. Give it a "5" if it includes most of them. Give it a "1" if it includes very few of them. Rate it somewhere in between if it has some of these friendly features.

table of contents	chapter introductions	margin notes
key terms highlighted	pictures	index
headings	study questions	graphs
signal words	glossary	subheadings
chapter summaries	charts	list of key facts

1	2	3	4	5
VERY UNFRIENDLY			VERY FRIENDLY	

Friendliness Rating: _____

= Language: "How difficult is the language in my reading assignment?"

Choose three paragraphs from different parts of your assignment. Read each paragraph out loud. Give your assignment a "5" if the paragraphs have no new words and mostly comfortable sentences. Give it a "1" if the paragraphs have many new words and mostly complicated sentences.

1	2	3	4	5
VERY DIFFICULT			VERY EASY	

Language Rating: _____

FLIP Chart

(continued)

I = *Interest: "How interesting is my reading assignment?"*

Skim your assignment. Read the title, introduction, headings, subheadings, and summary. Look at the pictures and graphics. Give it a "5" if you can't wait to read the whole thing. Give it a "1" if it looks boring to you—if you're really going to have to work to concentrate on it.

1	2	3	4	5
NOT INTERESTING			VERY INTERESTING	

Interest Rating: _____

P = *Prior Knowledge: "What do I already know about the material covered in my reading assignment?"*

Think about the title, introduction, headings, subheadings, and summary. Give your assignment a "5" if it's old news to you. Give it a "1" if you've never heard of the subject before now.

1	2	3	4	5
NOT FAMILIAR			VERY FAMILIAR	

Prior Knowledge Rating: _____

Scoring
Add up your ratings to find your overall rating:

Interpreting Your Score
17–20 rating points: The reading level should feel *comfortable* to you.
12–16 rating points: The reading level should feel *somewhat comfortable* to you.
 4–11 rating points: The reading level may feel *uncomfortable* to you.

FLIP Chart

Follow-Up

1. My purpose for reading is (circle one):

    a. for personal pleasure

    b. to prepare for class discussions

    c. to answer written questions for class assignments or homework

    d. to prepare for a test

    e. other: _____

2. My reading rate should be (circle one):

    a. slow (allowing time for rereading if necessary)

    b. medium (careful and analytical)

    c. rapid (steady, skipping sections that contain information I already know)

3. My reading budget is:

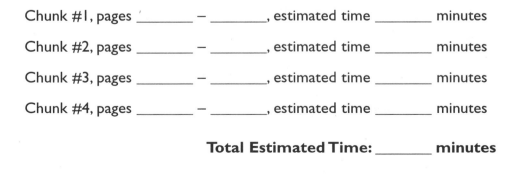

    Chunk #1, pages _____ – _____, estimated time _____ minutes

    Chunk #2, pages _____ – _____, estimated time _____ minutes

    Chunk #3, pages _____ – _____, estimated time _____ minutes

    Chunk #4, pages _____ – _____, estimated time _____ minutes

                      Total Estimated Time: _____ minutes

Guide for Story Reading

Step 1: Get Ready

• **Read the title page.**

• **Skim through the book looking at illustrations.**

• **Answer these questions:**

What is the title of the story? _____

Who is the author of the story? _____

Who is the illustrator of the story? _____

What is the setting of the story? _____

What time in history does the story take place? _____

Where does the story take place? _____

What do I predict this story will be about? _____

Step 2: Get Set

• **Read the first few pages or first chapter.**

• **Identify the main characters in the story.**

• **Answer these questions:**

Who are the main characters in the story? _____

_____

_____

What do you know about these characters? _____

_____

_____

_____ **More))**

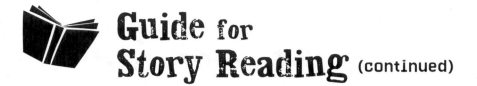

Guide for Story Reading (continued)

Step 3: Go

• **Read the rest of the story or the next chapter.**

• **Stop from time to time while reading to summarize what's going on and how you're reacting to the story.**

Step 4: Cool Down

• **Think about what you read.**

• **Answer these questions:**

What were the key events that happened in this story? _____

_____

_____

What part of the story did you like best? _____

_____

_____

What part of the story did you like least? _____

_____

_____

Would you recommend this story to a friend? Why or why not? _____

_____

_____

Step 5: Follow Up

Think about how to follow up with this book. _____

_____

_____

50 Fantastic Ideas for Book Sharing

1. List ten characters in the book.

2. List five characters and next to each name, write the character's occupation.

3. How old do you think the main character is? Why? Name three things the character does that match with that age.

4. If you could meet one of the characters, who would it be? List five questions you'd like to ask him or her. What answers do you think you'd receive?

5. Choose a character who made an important decision. Describe the situation.

6. Describe what one of the characters might eat for lunch. Why did you select such a menu?

7. List five characters from the book. Give each a nickname and tell why you chose it.

8. Find an example of stress or frustration by one of the characters. Tell about it. How did the character resolve it?

9. Do you think the main character would like a job at a local fast-food restaurant? Why or why not?

10. Would you choose the main character as your best friend? Why or why not?

11. Pick your favorite character. Give at least three reasons for your choice.

12. Pick your favorite and least favorite characters in the book. Give reasons why these characters could or could not be your friends.

13. Write a letter of advice to one of the characters.

14. Dress up as one of the characters or make a mask of the character.

15. Bring in props mentioned in the book and put on a play for your class.

16. Your favorite character has just been granted three wishes (none of the wishes may be for more wishes). Tell what she or he would wish for and why.

17. It's your favorite character's birthday. What gifts would you bring to the party?

18. Your favorite character just bought a T-shirt. Draw a picture of the T-shirt. Explain the picture.

19. One of the characters has a problem. Describe it and tell how it was solved.

20. Make a diary entry that your favorite character might write.

21. Act out various scenes in the book.

22. Make a video about one of the scenes in the book. You may want to have friends and family help with this assignment.

More))

23. Pick seven events that happen in the book and write them on a time line or draw them in a cartoon strip.

24. List five events that happen in the book in chronological order.

25. Write a follow-up chapter to the book.

26. In what season does the book take place? Give supporting statements.

27. Would you like to live in the setting (time and place) of this book? Why or why not?

28. List different kinds of transportation mentioned in the book.

29. Use a blank world or U.S. map to locate settings in the book.

30. Compare and contrast objects used in the setting of the book to what we use today.

31. Find examples of feelings in the book—love, guilt, honesty, trust, loneliness.

32. Find examples of humor in the book.

33. Survey ten students from your class. Ask them two opinion questions about the book. Record your results.

34. Write a poem about the book.

35. Write a rap about the book.

36. Write a song about the book.

37. Read your favorite part as if you were a radio announcer. Tape record your reading.

38. If your book were made into a movie, who would you select to play the various roles? You may pick friends or famous people.

39. Read a selection from the book to two friends and one family member. Write about their reactions.

40. Think up a dozen questions and answers about the book. Create a board game using the questions.

41. Make up three essay questions and answers that would be good for the end-of-the-book test.

42. Write to the book's publisher or author and tell what you think about the book.

43. Make up ten interview questions you'd like to ask the author.

44. Think of a new title for the book. Why did you choose it?

45. Create a title for each chapter.

46. Look up the author in a reference book. Tell five things you learned about this person.

47. Keep a Wonderful Word List. When you come to a new word or a unique saying or phrase, write it down.

48. Find three examples of onomatopoeia (words that resemble a sound, like *moo, hiss, cluck, slam*).

49. Draw a picture of the home or place where the main character lives.

50. Come up with your own activity.

Guide for Reading Informational Text

Reading assignment: _____

Topic: _____

Step 1: Preview

• **Look over pictures, charts, and graphs.**

• **Quickly read the instructions, headings, subheadings, and summary.**

• **Answer these questions:**

What do I know about this topic? _____

_____

_____

What do I think I'm going to learn about this topic? _____

_____

_____

Step 2: Action Reading

• **Read the assignment, one section at a time.**

• **After each section, identify and fix up "clunks" (difficult or confusing words or ideas).**

• **List two or three key ideas.**

Section 1

Clunks: _____

Key ideas: _____

_____

More ⟩⟩

Guide for Reading Informational Text (continued)

Section 2

Clunks: _____

Key ideas:_____

_____

Section 3

Clunks: _____

Key ideas:_____

_____

Section 4

Clunks: _____

Key ideas:_____

_____

Step 3: Wrap Up

• **Think about the whole passage you read.**

• **Talk about the most important ideas.**

Most important ideas: _____

_____

_____

• **Predict five or six questions the teacher might ask on a test.**

_____   _____

_____   _____

_____   _____

WRITING IDEAS

from A to Z

A
ad
advice column
autobiography

B
bedtime story
brochure
bumper sticker

C
cartoon
cereal box
CD cover

D
diary
directory
drama

E
editorial
email message
encyclopedia

F
fable
fashion article
fortune

G
game rule
graffiti
greeting card

H
headline
horoscope
how-to article

I
infomercial
interview
invitation

J
job description
joke
journal

K
keynote speech
kiddie story
knock-knock joke

L
legend
letter
limerick

M
menu
movie review
mystery

N
newspaper
notice
nursery rhyme

O
obituary
ode
ordinance

P
party plan
play
postcard

Q
questionnaire
quiz
quotation

R
recipe
rhyme
riddle

S
sign
song
sports story

T
thank-you note
travel brochure
TV program

U
up-to-the-minute
    news story
urgent notice

V
villanelle
visiting card
vivid verbs

W
weather forecast
Web site
wish

X
X-ray results

Y
yarn
yearbook

Z
zany tale
Zen koan
zoo map

✔ A-OK Checklist

Title: _____

Name of author: _____

Name of editor: _____

MOK (Meaning OK?)

	YES	NO
"Does it make sense?"	☐	☐
"Is it concise and to the point?"	☐	☐
"Is it complete?"	☐	☐
"Does it say what I really want to say?"	☐	☐
"Are my facts correct?"	☐	☐
"Is there an introduction?"	☐	☐
"Is there a conclusion?"	☐	☐

POK (Paragraph OK?)

	YES	NO
"Is it indented?"	☐	☐
"Is it made up of sentences related to *one* main idea?"	☐	☐
"Is it connected logically with paragraphs that come before or after?"	☐	☐

SOK (Sentence OK?)

	YES	NO
"Does it start with a capital letter?"	☐	☐
"Does it end with the correct punctuation mark?"	☐	☐

	YES	NO
"Is other punctuation used correctly?"	☐	☐
"Is it a complete sentence?"	☐	☐
"Does it express a complete thought?"	☐	☐
"Do the subject and verb agree?"	☐	☐
"Is its meaning clear?"	☐	☐

WOK (Word OK?)

	YES	NO
"Is it spelled correctly?"	☐	☐
"Is it capitalized correctly?"	☐	☐
"Is it used correctly?"	☐	☐
"Is it overused?"	☐	☐
"Is it slang?"	☐	☐
"Is it the *very best* word?"	☐	☐

NOK (Neatness OK?)

	YES	NO
"Does it follow the required format?"	☐	☐
"Have I used my best handwriting?"	☐	☐

Story Map

Setting

Time: _____

Place: _____

Characters

Name: _____

Description: _____

_____

_____

_____

_____

Name: _____

Description: _____

_____

_____

_____

_____

Name: _____

Description: _____

_____

_____

_____

_____

More ⟩⟩

Story Map (continued)

Events

1. _____
_____
_____

2. _____
_____
_____

3. _____
_____
_____

4. _____
_____
_____

5. _____
_____
_____

Problems _____
_____
_____
_____

Solutions_____
_____
_____
_____

I. Introduction

a. Title of book: _____

b. Author: _____

c. Type of book (examples: mystery, adventure, fantasy): _____

d. Setting of book _____

      Time: _____

      Place: _____

e. Why I read this book: _____

II. Characters

a. Main character (name and description): _____

_____

_____

_____

_____

b. Other important characters (names and descriptions): _____

_____

_____

_____

_____

_____

_____

_____

_____

`More ››`

Book Report: Fiction (continued)

III. Summary of plot

_____

_____

_____

_____

_____

_____

IV. Critique

a. The part I liked best was: _____

_____

_____

b. The part I liked least was: _____

_____

_____

c. This book was (check one)

☐ hard to read

☐ easy to read

☐ in between

d. I (check one)

☐ would

☐ would not

recommend this book to someone else because: _____

_____

_____

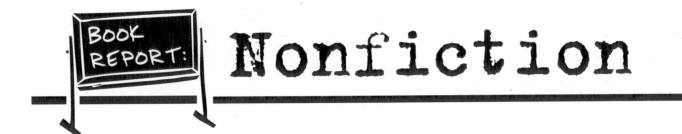

BOOK REPORT: Nonfiction

I. Introduction

a. Title of book: _____

b. Author: _____

c. Subject of book: _____

d. Why I read this book: _____

_____

_____

_____

_____

II. Summary of Book

_____

_____

_____

_____

_____

_____

_____

_____

_____

_____

_____

More ⟩⟩

Book Report: Nonfiction (continued)

III. New and interesting facts I learned from reading this book

_____

_____

_____

_____

_____

_____

IV. Critique

a. The part I liked best was: _____

_____

_____

b. The part I liked least was: _____

_____

_____

c. This book was (check one)

☐ hard to read

☐ easy to read

☐ in between

d. I (check one)

☐ would

☐ would not

recommend this book to someone else because: _____

_____

_____

I. Introduction

a. Title of book: _____

b. Author: _____

c. Subject of book: _____

d. Why I read this book: _____

_____

_____

_____

II. Summary of Book

a. What I learned about this person's life: _____

_____

_____

_____

_____

b. What I learned about this person's major achievements: _____

_____

_____

_____

_____

_____

_____

_____ **More >>**

Book Report: Biography (continued)

III. Problems

a. The major problem in this person's life was: _____

_____

b. How this problem was solved: _____

_____

IV. Why this person is remembered or admired today

_____

_____

V. Critique

a. The part I liked best was: _____

_____

b. The part I liked least was: _____

_____

c. This book was (check one)

☐ hard to read

☐ easy to read

☐ in between

d. I (check one)

☐ would

☐ would not

recommend this book to someone else because: _____

_____

_____

✔ Research Paper Checklist

Assignment: To write a term paper on _____

_____

_____

_____

_____

Due date: _____

Requirements:

My paper will need:

- [ ] title page
- [ ] table of contents
- [ ] bibliography
- [ ] graphics (If so, what kind of graphics?)

It should be:

- [ ] typed
- [ ] double-spaced
- [ ] handwritten

Steps: DATE DUE   DATE DONE

1. Choose a topic.   _____   _____

2. Write a thesis sentence. Get it approved by the teacher.   _____   _____

3. Do library research.   _____   _____

Sources:

_____

_____

_____

_____

_____

More ⟩⟩

Research Paper Checklist (continued)

	DATE DUE	DATE DONE

4. Check the Internet for additional information. _____ _____

Web sites:

_____

_____

_____

5. Contact community resources for information. _____ _____

Names of resources:

_____

_____

_____

6. Write letters to request information from national sources. _____ _____

Wrote letters to:

_____

_____

_____

7. Take Notes. _____ _____

Took notes from these sources:

_____

_____

_____

8. Make a writing plan. _____ _____

9. Write a rough draft. _____ _____

10. Revise and edit rough draft; make corrections. _____ _____

11. Write the final draft. _____ _____

12. Turn in the final draft on time. _____ _____

Spelling Demons

about	decorate	know	receive	though
address	didn't	laid	received	thought
advise	doctor	latter	remember	through
again	does	lessons	right	tired
all right	early	letter	rough	together
along	Easter	little	route	tomorrow
already	easy	loose	said	tonight
although	enough	loving	Santa Claus	too
always	every	making	Saturday	toys
among	everybody	many	says	train
April	favorite	maybe	school	traveling
arithmetic	February	minute	schoolhouse	trouble
aunt	fierce	morning	several	truly
awhile	first	mother	shoes	Tuesday
balloon	football	name	since	two
because	forty	neither	skiing	until
been	fourth	nice	skis	used
before	Friday	none	some	vacation
birthday	friend	o'clock	something	very
blue	fuel	off	sometime	wear
bought	getting	often	soon	weather
built	goes	once	store	weigh
busy	grade	outside	straight	we're
buy	guard	party	studying	were
children	guess	peace	sugar	when
chocolate	half	people	summer	where
choose	Halloween	piece	Sunday	which
Christmas	handkerchief	played	suppose	white
close	haven't	plays	sure	whole
color	having	please	surely	women
come	hear	poison	surprise	would
coming	heard	practice	surrounded	write
cough	height	pretty	swimming	writing
could	hello	principal	teacher	wrote
couldn't	here	quarter	tear	you
country	hospital	quit	terrible	you're
cousin	hour	quite	Thanksgiving	your
cupboard	house	raise	their	
dairy	instead	read	there	
dear	knew	ready	they	

Spelling Demons II

absence	conceive	grammar	opportunity	seize
acceptable	condemn	guarantee	paid	sense
accommodate	conscience	guidance	parallel	separate
accustom	conscientious	height	paralyzed	sergeant
ache	conscious	heroes	particular	shining
achievement	controversial	hypocrite	performance	similar
acquire	controversy	incredible	personal	sincerely
across	council	interest	personnel	sophomore
adolescent	criticize	interrupt	pleasant	stationary
advantageous	definitely	irrelevant	politician	studying
advertisement	definition	its	portrayed	substantial
advice	descendant	jealousy	possession	subtle
against	describe	led	possible	succeed
aisle	description	leisurely	practical	succession
amateur	desert	license	preferred	supersede
analyze	dilemma	lieutenant	prejudice	surprise
annually	diligence	listener	prepare	susceptible
anticipated	dining	lose	prescription	technique
apparent	disastrous	luxury	prestige	thorough
appreciate	discipline	magnificent	prevalent	tragedy
arctic	disease	maneuver	principal	transferred
arguing	dissatisfied	marriage	principle	tremendous
argument	effect	mathematics	privilege	unnecessary
arrangement	embarrass	medicine	probably	vacuum
athlete	emigrate	mere	procedure	valuable
bargain	endeavor	miniature	proceed	vegetable
belief	environment	miscellaneous	profession	vengeance
beneficial	especially	mischief	professor	villain
benefited	exaggerate	moral	prominent	visible
breathe	exceed	muscle	pursue	waive
Britain	except	mysterious	quiet	woman
bury	exercise	necessary	receipt	wrench
business	exhausted	niece	receive	write
calendar	existence	noticeable	recommend	writing
category	experience	numerous	referring	yacht
cemetery	explanation	occasion	renowned	
certainly	fascinate	occurred	repetition	
cite	formerly	occurrence	restaurant	
comparative	gaiety	occurring	rhythm	
concede	gauge	opinion	saucer	

 **Study Checkup**

Record the number of minutes you spend on each study activity. Do this for one study session, or a week's worth. Find out how you're spending your time. Decide if you need to make changes in your study habits.

Today's Date: _____

Minutes Spent	**Study Activity**
_____	Getting ready to study
_____	Completing my homework assignments
_____	Checking my homework assignments
_____	Identifying and quizzing myself on important facts and terms
_____	Previewing the chapter(s)
_____	Active reading (outlining, taking notes, semantic mapping, summarizing, annotating, highlighting, making flash cards)
_____	Comparing chapter notes with a friend
_____	Quizzing myself on chapter notes
_____	Rewriting and revising chapter notes
_____	Comparing class notes with a friend
_____	Highlighting class notes
_____	Quizzing myself on class notes
_____	Reading extra material for background
_____	Merging class notes and chapter notes
_____	Making up sample test questions
_____	Taping my sample questions and answers
_____	Listening to my study tape
_____	Getting study materials together to take to school
_____	_____
_____	_____

What do I need to spend *more* time doing? _____

What do I need to spend *less* time doing? _____

Index

About the Author

Jeanne Shay Schumm, Ph.D., is professor and chair of the Department of Teaching and Learning in the School of Education at University of Miami. She teaches graduate courses in reading assessment and instruction and is actively engaged in research on reading. She has coauthored over 75 research articles.

Jeanne loves canoeing and camping. She paddled over 75 miles of the Mississippi River with her husband, Jerry (see page 20). Jeanne and Jerry have a daughter, Jamie, who lives in New Orleans with her husband, John, and their son, Jack.